Warehouse Theatre Company's

FEMME FATALE

Written by Phil Willmott
Directed by Ted Craig
Music by Phil Willmott and Stefan Bednarczyk
Designed by Ellen Cairns
Lighting by Matthew Eagland
Musical Staging by Darren Royston

Femme Fatale was commissioned by the Warehouse Theatre Company and the world premiere took place at the Warehouse Theatre, on Friday 10 December 2004

Warehouse Theatre Company Regd. Charity No: 272816

Femme Fatale

Cast

Delores	Rosie Jenkins
Joe	Jamie Read
Granger	Kit Benjamin
Irwin	Tim Frances
Estella	Elizabeth Marsh
Edgar	Tomm Coles

All other parts are played by members of the company
Music played live by the company

Written by	Phil Willmott
Directed by	Ted Craig
Music by	Phil Willmott Stefan Bednarczyk
Musical Direction	Stefan Bednarczyk
Designer	Ellen Cairns
Lighting Designer	Matthew Eagland
Musical Staging	Darren Royston
Production Manager	Graham Constable
Stage Manager	Ria Tubman
Assistant Stage Manager	Janie Morris
Casting	Sooki McShane
Press (national)	Guy Chapman Associates
(local)	Simon Reilly

Kit Benjamin

Kit has played a variety of weird and wonderful characters on stage, from a psychotic soldier in Kafka's *In The Prison Colony* to the androgynous role of Mary Sunshine in Century Theatre's national tour of *Chicago.* He also toured for the same company in a rare revival of Noel Coward's *Bitter Sweet*. West End credits include *Cats* at the New London Theatre and *Buddy* at the Strand Theatre. He also spent two years playing Pat Levin, a role which he created, in Paul Elliot's production of *Jolson,* starring Brian Conley, at the Victoria Palace Theatre and on tour in the UK and Canada.

More recently, Kit has appeared in *Wild Orchids* at Chichester Festival Theatre, and has become a veteran of the Dick Barton series here at the Warehouse Theatre, having appeared as the BBC Announcer in four out of the five episodes. Kit reached the pinnacle of his comedy career this April, when he was employed to rip John McEnroe's shirt off at the *Laureus World Sports Awards*.

Kit is delighted to be back at the Warehouse again this year.

Jamie Read

Jamie is from a musical family, and made his debut aged eight playing Judi Dench's son in *Entertaining Strangers*, at the National Theatre! His theatre credits include the RSC's *Wizard of Oz* (Barbican, London); Prince Alfred in *Joy to the World* and The Knight in *St. Georges Day Pageant* (Royal Albert Hall/BBC), Charlie in *Marvin's Room* (Hampstead Theatre and West End), *Aladdin* (Perth Theatre, Scotland); Lero The Great in the original workshop of *Hard Times The Musical* (Union Chapel, Islington); Ensemble & understudied/played Danny Boy in *Spirit of The Dance* (European tour and US productions); *Hard Times The Musical*, reprising the role of Lero The Great and understudied/played Tom Gradgrind (Windsor & Theatre Royal Haymarket); Benjamin in *Joseph and The Amazing Technicolor Dreamcoat* (UK national tour, plus many subsequent return visits to the show in the West End); *La Belle Hélène* for the Castleward Opera Season (Castleward National Trust House, Belfast); Bosie/Narrator in *The Ballad of Reading Gaol*, for which Jamie also co-wrote the music and was nominated in the British Composers

Awards (Edinburgh Festival); and Emperor Wu in *The Emperor & The Nightingale* at the MAC, Birmingham.
TV/Film: Irish Dancer in *The Boys From County Clare*; Jeff in the short film *Renée*; and Franz Gockel in the BBC's highly acclaimed documentary/drama *D-Day*. Also, for children's TV: *Playbus* (BBC); and *T-Bag* (Thames). Original cast recordings include *The Wizard of Oz*; *Hard Times – The Musical*; *The Ballad of Reading Gaol*; and also the soundtrack to the movie *The Boys From County Clare*.
Jamie also works as a choreographer and teacher, and runs his own adult dance centre in his home town of Reading.

Rosie Jenkins

Rosie trained at the Guildford School of Acting. Most recently, she has appeared as April in *Company* at the New Wolsey Theatre, Ipswich, prior to that appearing as Swallow in No 1 National Tour of *Whistle Down the Wind* (Bill Kenwright Productions). Rosie was born and grew up in Brighton where she appeared, aged four, in New Sussex Opera's production of *Peter Grimes* and again the following year in *The Queen of Spades*. Subsequent theatre work includes: Maria in *West Side Story* (Connaught Theatre, Worthing); Victoria in *Follow that Girl* and Amelia in *Vanity Fair* (both Theatre Museum, Covent Garden); Original London cast of *Zippertydoodah*, *100 Musicals in 100 Minutes* (with Gyles Brandreth, New Wimbledon Theatre); *In the Red* (Her Majesty's Theatre, Haymarket); Snow White in *Snow White and the Seven Dwarves* (Playhouse Theatre, Weston Super Mare; Artslink Theatre, Camberley; Watersmeet Theatre, Rickmansworth and Palace Theatre, Redditch); Claudette Orbison in Bill Kenwright's *The Roy Orbison Story* (National No1 Tour 2003). Television work includes: *My Family, On the Straight and Narrow, Crime Watch*, and *Songs of Praise,* all for the BBC. Rosie plays the trumpet and has just taken up the sax!

Tomm Coles

After completing a degree in Drama with French at Hull University, Tomm trained at The Royal Welsh College of Music and Drama. Recent theatre credits include Tybalt in Terry Hands' *Romeo and Juliet* (Clwyd Theatre Cymru, Mold) Roger in *Silence* (Sherman Theatre, Cardiff), Levi in *Joseph and the Amazing Technicolor Dreamcoat,* and Angelo in *The Comedy of Errors* (Stafford Shakespeare Festival 2004)

Other theatre credits include : Yepikhodov in *The Cherry Orchard*, Le Chevalier Danceny in *Les Liaisons Dangereuses*, Don Pedro in *Much Ado about Nothing*, and Clifford Bradshaw in *Cabaret*.

Tomm has performed at the Edinburgh Festival and appeared in a number of short films as well as working in HMP Pentonville with Bruce Wall on the Animated Macbeth Project.

Tim Frances

Theatre includes: *Proving Mr Jennings* (Courtyard Theatre), *An Inspector Calls* (West End & on tour), *Marat-Sade* (Royal National Theatre), *Sleeping Beauty* (Northampton Royal Theatre), *Habeas Corpus* (Salisbury Playhouse), *Romeo & Juliet* (Greenwich Theatre), *The Nun* (Greenwich Studio Theatre), *Aladdin* (Liverpool Everyman), *Cabaret*, *Jungle Book*, *A Comedy of Errors,* and *A Christmas Carol* (Lancaster Duke's Playhouse), *June Moon* (Theatre of Comedy at the Vaudeville, West End), *King Lear* (Compass Theatre with Anthony Quayle), *Coriolanus* (USA & Canada), *Freedom To Forget* and *Treasure Island* (Farnham Redgrave), *One-Eyed Monster* (Greenwich Theatre), *I Bertolt Brecht* (Good Company), *Macbeth* (New Cross Theatre), *Good Rockin' Tonite* (Bill Kenwright tour) and *Barnstormers* (Century Theatre, UK & India tour).

Television includes: *What If...Drugs Were Legal* (showing December BBC), *Bad Girls*, *My Dad's the Prime Minister, The Inspector Lynley Mysteries, Cromwell, Holby City*, *East Enders*, *The Bill*, *Doctors*, *Lexx*, *Scar Stories*, *To Hell & Back*, *Search*, and Andrew Davies' *Othello.*

Radio: readings of Browning & Tennyson for the BBC, two series of short stories, and *She Fell Among Thieves* (BBC R4). Film: *Three Men In A Restaurant* with Dexter Fletcher and Jack Davenport is due for

release...some time ... Also *Panther Walk*, *Likely Story* and *The Taming of the Shrew* (Petruchio). Coming up, *Berenice* – from the Edgar Allan Poe story.
As pianist and arranger, Tim has played with jazz ensembles *Man Made Souls* and *Does It Matter?*

Elizabeth Marsh
Elizabeth trained at the Guildford School of Acting. She has performed at the National Theatre, in the West End and at many repertory theatres around the country.
Favourite roles include: Ymma in *Silence*; Jenny in *The Threepenny Opera*; Betty in *Blonde Bombshells of 1943*; Susan in *Company*; Cassilda in *Gondoliers*; Anne Wilkes in *Misery*; Beverly in *Abigail's Party*; Miss Hannigan in *Annie*; Jean Rice in *The Entertainer*; Rose in *Brighton Rock*; Louisa in *Hard Times*; Suzanne in *Don't Dress for Dinner*; Rita in *In the Midnight Hour;* Mrs Kay in *Our Day Out*; Pamela in *The 39 Steps*; Fabia in *Twelfth Night*; Yitzak in *Hedwig and the Angry Inch* and Mme Giry in *Phantom of the Opera*.
Elizabeth has also worked on numerous musicals, pantomimes and revues as a choreographer; most recently *Pinafore Swing* for the Watermill Theatre, Newbury and tour.

Phil Willmott – Writer

Phil studied Theatre Arts at Rose Bruford College and is a director, playwright and performer.
He is delighted that Ted Craig is producing their latest collaboration at the Warehouse. As it opens he will be directing Lesley Joseph in *Snow White* at Newcastle's Theatre Royal and his radical *London Nativity* at The Scoop Amphitheatre on the South Bank.
He has directed over forty productions around the UK from Shakespeare and musicals to cutting edge new writing. He is Artistic Director of his own multi award winning theatre company The Steam Industry (incorporating The Finborough Theatre and The Scoop) and was an Associate Artist of London's acclaimed Battersea Arts Centre throughout the 1990s.
Past successful productions have included Athol Fugard's *Master Harold...and the boys* and his own musical of *Around the World in Eighty Days* at Liverpool Playhouse, *Rent* at the Olympia in Dublin, *Pal Joey* at Nottingham Playhouse, *Angels in America* at Sheffield Crucible, *Oedipus, Agamemnon* and *Androcles and the Lion* at the Scoop and many other acclaimed Off West End productions including all of the BAC Christmas musicals, the world premiere of Germaine Greer's *Lysistrata,* the Bridewell UK premiere of *Victor/Victoria*, Shakespeare's *Henry VIII, Measure for Measure* & *Titus Andronicus* and Brecht's *Arturo Ui* plus four shows as either playwright or director at the Yvonne Arnaud Theatre in Guildford where he was Associate Director.
As a writer many of his plays, musicals and adaptations have been published and are regularly produced around the world, including the first three episodes of *Dick Barton.*

Ted Craig – Director

Ted's career has included the directorship of the Drama Theatre of the Sydney Opera House and many freelance productions both here and abroad. These include the Off-Broadway production of *Look Back in Anger* with Malcolm McDowell (Roundabout Theatre); *The Astronomer's Garden* by Kevin Hood (Warehouse and Royal Court Theatre); *Playing Sinatra* by Bernard Kops (Warehouse and Hampstead Theatre); Shakespeare's *The Tempest*; Congreve's *Love for Love*, Molière's *The Misanthrope* and Feydeau's *The Lady from Maxim's* (Sydney Opera House); *Tarantara Tarantara! by* Ian Taylor (Theatre Royal, Sydney and Australian tour); *The Elephant Man* by Bernard Pomerance (Melbourne

Theatre Company) and Arthur Miller's *The Last Yankee* and Joe Orton's *Entertaining Mr Sloane* (Theatro Ena, Cyprus), *Blood Royal* by Charles Thomas at the King's Head Theatre and *Skin Deep* at the Warehouse Theatre. He commissioned the Dick Barton series and directed each one of the five episodes. He co-founded the International Playwriting Festival and is proud of its considerable achievements in discovering and promoting new playwrights over the past 19 years. Ted is the Artistic Director and Chief Executive of the Warehouse Theatre Company.

Stefan Bednarczyk – Musical Director

Theatre credits as an actor include: *"ZIP!"* (National Tour), *The Glee Club* (Bush Theatre tour), *Semi-monde* (Lyric Theatre, Shaftesbury Avenue); *Dick Barton – Special Agent* (Warehouse Theatre, Croydon); *Whenever* (Stephen Joseph Theatre); *Jermyn Street Revue* (Jermyn Street Theatre); *5 o'clock Angel* (Edinburgh, Hampstead, King's Head Theatres); *Laughter on the 23rd Floor* (Queen's Theatre, London and national tour); *Schippel the Plumber* (Greenwich); *The LA Plays* (Almeida); *The Game of Love and Chance* (Royal National Theatre); *Sugar Hill Blues* (Warehouse Theatre, Hampstead); *Playing Sinatra* (Warehouse Theatre, Greenwich); *A Midsummer Night's Dream* (Leicester); *A Midsummer Night's Dream* and *Twelfth Night* (Regent's Park); *Mozart and Salieri* (ATC); *Merrily We Roll Along* and *Noel and Gertie* (Cardiff); *Robert and Elizabeth* (Chichester); *Last Song Of The Nightingale* (Edinburgh & Greenwich). Musical direction has included shows at Chichester. Cardiff, Swansea, Leeds, Sheffield, Oxford and Regent's Park Open Air Theatre, Holder's Opera Festival (Barbados), Warehouse Theatre, Croydon and, together with Judy Campbell, *Where Are The Songs We Sung* (Kings Head Theatre). Television credits include: *Crocodile Shoes*, *Crown Prosecutor*, *EastEnders*, *Love Hurts*, *Paul Merton – The Series*, *Harry Enfield and Chums*, *Stefan's Guide to Culture*, *The Grand Style of Old Jazz*. Solo cabaret performances include seasons in London (Pizza on the Park, King's Head Theatre, Jermyn Street Theatre), throughout the UK and abroad in Cannes, Antibes, San Francisco, Barbados, Monaco, Cologne, New York, Los Angeles, Vienna and Adelaide Festival. Film credits include: *Topsy-Turvy*, *Composed* and *Sea Change*. Stefan was also Musical Director of *Dick Barton – Special Agent* since the first production.

Ellen Cairns – Designer

Ellen Cairns trained at Glasgow School of Art and The Slade. Her last production at the Warehouse Theatre was *Knock Down Ginger*, having previously worked with its Artistic Director Ted Craig on *Dick Barton: Flight of the Phoenix* in 2002 and *Happy & Glorious* in 1999. She designs extensively in this country and abroad; recent credits including: *Educating Rita* (Liverpool Playhouse); *Les Miserables* (Estonia); Arthur Koestler's *Darkness at Noon* (Stockholm Stadsteater); *Moon on a Rainbow Shawl* (Nottingham Playhouse) *Bent – a Cabaret* (Tallinn) and *West Side Story* (Finland). She also designed *Miss Saigon* in Helsinki and *My Fair Lady* for the Estonian National Opera.

Matthew Eagland – Lighting Designer

Matthew has created lighting designs for many productions such as *Little Women* (Duchess Theatre), *Anne of Green Gables* (Lilian Baylis Theatre), *Dancing at Lughnasa* (Northcott Exeter), *Much Ado About Nothing* (Bremer Shakespeare Company), *Christmas*(The Bush Theatre), *The Lieutenant of Inishmore* (National Tour), *Darwin in Malibu* (Birmingham Rep) and *Moon on a Rainbow Shawl* (Nottingham Playhouse).
Matthew has also lit many shows at the Tricycle and for the Queen's Theatre Hornchurch, the Oxford Stage Company, the Bath Shakespeare Festival, the National Youth Theatre, Southwark Playhouse, the Gate, Guildhall School of Music and Drama, and English Touring Opera (Education).

Darren Royston – Musical Staging

Darren works freelance in TV, Film, Opera, Theatre and Musicals. Credits in 2004 include choreography for *Into the Woods* (RADA), *On the Razzle* (RADA), *Coriolanus* (RADA), *Fred and Ginger* (ARTS), *Murder in Surburbia* (Carlton TV).
Director/Choreographer for European Chamber Opera 2004 Productions, *Don Pasquale* (Hever Castle), *Cosi Fan tutte, Tosca, Rigoletto* (Far East & Middle East Tour). Darren teaches dance and period movement at RADA and appears in the new Mike Leigh Film *Vera Drake* dancing the quickstep.

Ria Tubman – Stage Manager

Ria trained at Middlesex University with a BA (Hons) degree in Drama and Technical theatre. Since graduating, Ria has been working at the Royal Opera House as a lighting technician. Ria has also been working as a freelance stage manager for three years at such theatres as the Crucible and the Lyceum in Sheffield and the Buxton Opera House. She has also stagemanaged at music festivals including Glastonbury.

Janie Morris – Assistant Stage Manager

Janie studied at the College of West Anglia with a National Diploma in Performing Arts (Technical). Whilst at college, she worked on over 50 productions ranging in all aspects of stage management. She has worked at the National Theatre as Deputy Stage Manager and at C Venues during the Edinburgh Fringe. This is Janie's first production with the Warehouse Theatre.

Graham Constable – Production Manager

Graham studied Stage Design and Performance at the Rijiksakademie, Amsterdam and under Josef Szajkna at the Studio Theatre, Warsaw. He returned to London and formed ARC, a mixed media performance group. Graham has constructed properties for film, television and theatre, for companies as diverse as BBC TV, Venezuelan TV, The Edinburgh Wax Museum and Glyndebourne Opera. As the Warehouse Theatre's Production Manager, he has built over forty-five shows.

Founded in 1977 in one of Croydon's few remaining Victorian industrial buildings, a national reputation was soon built for producing and presenting the best in new writing. In 1986 the prestigious International Playwriting Festival was launched. Having inaugurated a partnership with the leading Italian playwriting festival, the Premio Candoni Arta Terme, in 1995, selected plays are now seen in Italy offering the potential for further performance opportunities in Europe. A partnership has also been formed with Theatro Ena in Cyprus. Previous winners – such as Kevin Hood, whose play *Beached* won the first ever Festival – have gone on to achieve incredible success nationally and internationally. Kevin's two subsequent plays for the Warehouse, *The Astronomer's Garden* and *Sugar Hill Blues,* both transferred, the first to the Royal Court and the second to Hampstead Theatre.

Today the Warehouse Theatre is acknowledged as one of the foremost theatres for new playwriting in the country. Other hugely successful productions have included *Sweet Phoebe,* by Australian playwright Michael Gow, which saw the London stage debut of Cate Blanchett, *Iona Rain* (winner of the 1995 International Playwriting Festival) and *The Blue Garden,* both by acclaimed playwright Peter Moffat, and the critically acclaimed *The Dove* by Bulgarian playwright Roumen Shomov. A huge success of the company is the stage version of *Dick Barton – Special Agent*. First produced at the Warehouse in December 1998 it was an instant success, was brought back by popular demand in 1999 and then toured nationally. More success then followed with a further four episodes, all premiered at the Warehouse Theatre.

The theatre is also proud of its partnership with other companies who share the commitment to new work, discovering and promoting the fledgling Frantic Assembly and other companies like Red Shift, Theatre Alibi, Look Out Theatre and Hijinks. Longstanding partnerships with Black Theatre Co-op (now Nitro) and Tara Arts have been in the forefront of the theatre's commitment to access and equality.

A culturally diverse education project in May–July 2003, based on issues raised in the production of *Knock Down Ginger* by Mark Norfolk, has been hailed as a groundbreaking success in forging new links between the education and arts sector. The education project was nominated for Arts Council England's Eclipse Award for combating racism through theatre in September 2003 and writer Mark Norfolk won the Croydon Champion award for Culture December 2003.

The Warehouse Theatre Company also runs a thriving Writers Workshop programme and a lively youth group and stages plays for younger children every Saturday.

Warehouse Theatre

Artistic Director	Ted Craig
Administrative Director	Evita Bier
Marketing Manager	Simon Reilly
Assistant Administrator	Rachel Farlie
Education Manager	Rose Marie Vernon
Box Office Manager	Leni Robson
Production Manager	Graham Constable
Literary Associate	Richard Vincent
Box Office	Rachael Jones, Deepak Raj, Francesca Burgoyne, Alison Salmon
Front Of House	Margaret Hicks, Adrienne Soloman, Mark Williams, Ian Suter, Catherine Bryden, Alice Elfer, Matthew Rangecroft, Arlene Smith, Ada Simpson

Board of Management
John Ball (Chair), Cllr Eddy Arram, Celia Bannerman, John Clarke, Timothy Godfrey, Dr Jean Gooding MBE, Cllr Brenda Kirby, Dominic Parker, Malti Patel, Michael Rose, Cllr Martin Tiedmann, Cllr Mary Walker OBE

Patrons
Lord Attenborough CBE, George Baker, Lord Bowness CBE DL, John Gale OBE, Dame Joan Plowright, Robert Stiby JP

Funding Bodies

Sponsorship

The
Peggy
Ramsay
Foundation

The Warehouse Theatre Company's International Playwrighting Festival

A National and International Stage for New Writing

Celebrating nineteen years of success, the IPF continues to discover, nurture and promote the work of new playwrights.
The IPF is held in two parts – plays from all over the world are entered into the competition and judged by a panel of distinguished theatre practitioners. The best selected plays are then showcased at the Festival, which takes place every November. Entries for the competition are received from January. Plays are also presented in Italy at the leading playwriting festival Premio Candoni Arta Terme and many selected plays go on to production in Britain and abroad. International partners are Premio Candoni Arta Terme and Theatro Ena, Nicosia.

Recent Successes

Six Black Candles by Des Dillon (IPF 2001) premiere at the Royal Lyceum Theatre Edinburgh 2004.
Knock Down Ginger by Mark Norfolk (IPF 2001) premiered at the Premio Candoni Arta Terme 2002, was produced at Warehouse Theatre in June 2003 and his second play *Wrong Pace* was produced at Soho Theatre October 2003.
Red On Black by Andrew Bridgmont (IPF 2000) premiered at Hen & Chickens Theatre 2003.
The Dove by Bulgarian playwright Roumen Shomov (IPF 1999) produced at Warehouse Theatre in April 2000, was showcased at the Premio Candoni Arta Terme the same year, and went on to be produced twice in Bulgaria.
The Shagaround by Maggie Nevill (IPF 1999) was showcased in Italian at the Premio Candoni Arta Terme and at the Tricycle Theatre in English. The play, produced by the Warehouse Theatre Company and the Nuffield Theatre, Southampton has since toured at Nuffield Theatre (Southampton), Ashcroft Theatre (London), Soho Theatre (London) and Brighton Theatre Royal.
51 Peg by Phillip Edwards (IPF 1998) was showcased at the Premio Candoni Arta-Terme in Italy May 1999 and was produced at the Edinburgh Festival 2000.
The Resurrectionists by Dominic McHale (IPF 1997) premiered at Warehouse Theatre in 1998, as a co-production between the Warehouse Theatre Company and the Octagon Theatre, Bolton. It was also performed at the Octagon the same year.

Real Estate by Richard Vincent (IPF 1994) was produced in Italy by Il Centro per la Drammaturgia Contemporanea "H" and Beat 72 at Teatro Colosseo in Rome December 2001.
The selected plays for the IPF 2004 were *Weather* by Gary Baxter, *Smile Bloody Smile* by Andrew Heath, *Happy Talk* by Charlie Moore, *Surface* by Heather Taylor, *Ron's Pig Palace on Wheels* by Jennifer Tuckett, and *Someplace Else* by Imola Zsitva.

Knock Down Ginger

The Dove

The Shagaround

The Resurrectionists

Sweet Phoebe

First published in 2004 by Oberon Books Ltd.
521 Caledonian Road, London N7 9RH
Tel: 020 7607 3637 / Fax: 020 7607 3629

e-mail: oberon.books@btinternet.com
www.oberonbooks.com

Copyright © Phil Willmott 2004.

Phil Willmott is hereby identified as the author of this play in accordance with section 77 of the Copyright, Designs and Patents Act 1988. The author has asserted his moral rights.

All rights whatsoever in this play are strictly reserved and application for performance etc. should be made before commencement of rehearsal to Curtis Brown Group Ltd, Haymarket House, 28–29 Haymarket, London SW1Y 4SP. No performance may be given unless a licence has been obtained, and no alterations may be made in the title or the text of the play without the author's prior written consent.

This book is sold subject to the condition that it shall not by way of trade or otherwise be circulated without the publisher's consent in any form of binding or cover or circulated electronically other than that in which it is published and without a similar condition including this condition being imposed on any subsequent purchaser.

A catalogue record for this book is available from the British Library.

ISBN: 1 84002 535 2

Printed in Great Britain by Antony Rowe Ltd, Chippenham.

Characters

RAYMOND CHANDLER
EDITOR OF *THE CLARION*
DELORES
EDGAR
HOTEL MANAGER
JOE
GRANGER THE BUTLER
IRWIN
ESTELLA
OSWALD
MAXWELL
MANFRED
AXEL

Setting

A composite set that will allow the action to move without pause from scene to scene through multiple, simply-suggested locations.

Film Noir

The problem, or joy, of Film Noir is that it is not a genre that can be easily defined, but is a matter of tone and mood. The visual is often made up of layers of black and grey. The human characters are obsessed and are compelled to act in the way they do and the Femme Fatale is often at the centre of this obsession.

The look of Film Noir can be traced back to the German Expressionist cinema of the 1920s and 1930s. The ultimate example of this cinema is *The Cabinet of Dr Caligari (1919 d. Robert Wiene)* with its surreal settings, weird angles, montage, forced perspective and other technical innovations. But with the coming of sound the 'gothic' lighting style and Expressionist angles became difficult to manage because the equipment was so cumbersome and noisy.

Many film directors and their creative personnel escaped Hitler's Germany and hotfooted it to Hollywood. These included Fritz Lang, Billy Wilder, Robert Siodmak, Fred Zinnerman and Edgar G Ulmer. When they got there, what were they to film? Hollywood primarily films the best-selling books of the time and in the late 1930s and early 1940s these were hard-boiled novels by the likes of Dashiell Hammett and Raymond Chandler. The directors mined this raw material for their work and, as luck would have it, many of these authors lived in Los Angeles and liked making money writing film scripts. And as technological advances had brought lighter and more mobile cameras, the cinematographers and directors explored every opportunity.

But the sparse, single-source lighting style of Film Noir was also a product of necessity. The advent of World War Two meant the sales market for Hollywood movies had shrunk enormously. As a result budgets were reduced, and dark shadows were often employed to hide the fact that there was no set!

Ted Craig

Some notable Film Noirs:
They Drive By Night 40 Raoul Walsh
Stranger On The Third Floor 40 Boris Ingster
The Maltese Falcon 41 John Huston
Shadow Of A Doubt 43 Alfred Hitchcock
Double Indemnity 44 Billy Wilder
Detour 45 Edgar G Ulmer
Mildred Pierce 45 Michael Curtiz
Conflict 45 Curtis Bernhardt
The Big Sleep 46 Howard Hawks
Cross Fire 47 Edward Dmytryk
Out Of The Past 47 Jacques Tourneur
The Lady From Shanghai 48 Orson Welles
Force Of Evil 48 Abraham Polonsky
I Walk Alone 48 Byron Haskin
Key Largo 48 John Huston
Sorry Wrong Number 48 Anatole Litvak
Act Of Violence 49 Fred Zinnemann
Sunset Boulevard 50 Billy Wilder
DOA 50 Rudolf Maté
Pick Up On South Street 53 Samuel Fuller

Musical Numbers

Act One

MILDRED PEARCE
Delores

LOST AND FOUND
Joe

NURSE ESTELLA'S EXERCISE REGIME
Estella

THAT GIRL
Joe and Edgar

ADIOS!
Estella and Granger

Act Two

B PICTURE ACTING
Irwin, Oswald, Hotel Manager

THE COMPENSATION QUADRILLE
Claimants

I'M AN UNUSUAL GIRL
Estella and Maxwell

IN TWO MINDS
Edgar

I WANT TO BE YOUR BABY
Maxwell

For Tim, who first turned me on to this black and white thing.

ACT ONE

In the darkness we hear a Chandleresque Voice over.

A lonely saxophone underscores.

CHANDLER: (*Voice over.*) Welcome to Noir, a haunted, timeless place where shadows from the silver screen blend their black and white palate of glamour, desperation, heroism and despair.

Lights up on a newspaper EDITOR talking to the audience as if they were his reporters.

EDITOR: OK, listen up you shmucks, call yourself reporters? Today's *Clarion* was so dull I wouldn't grace my cat's litter tray with it. Jeez, we were so short of salacious dirt I was forced to print news! And that ain't natural. If the good Lord wanted us to take an interest in current affairs he'd give the president a rack like Mae West and a two hundred dollars a day coke habit. Well, I want tomorrow's edition to bite like a barracuda in a bath tub. I got a tip-off about some broad they're calling the Black Widow. She's been marrying lucky ageing millionaires all over the country then sending 'em back to their maker with a smile on their face and her name on their will. Now, no one's heard anything of her for a while, but police in five states wanna ask her some questions and she was last heard of heading this way. 'Course the cops here in Angel City couldn't find clams in chowder. So first person to come back with an exclusive on this one doesn't get fired!

Blackout.
Saxophone in again.

CHANDLER: (*Voice over.*) Soon the few midday shafts of sunlight are like some forgotten dream as the glow of neon flashes its dangers into the greasy puddles.

Beat.

Frank was alone and he liked it that way, he pulled his trench coat tight against the bitter wind and revelled in the solitude. Man has never really drunk deep of his loneliness till he's tasted the bitter-sweet tang of a city after dark.

Saxophone and rain abruptly out.

Suddenly a werewolf rounded the corner of 8th and grabbed him by the ankle –

Lights up on the living room area of a classy hotel suite.
Obligatory Venetian blind shadows.
RAYMOND CHANDLER sits with his back to us and suitcase by his side.
DELORES, a sweet young chambermaid has disturbed him. She's a dumb, maybe breathy but not squeaky, blonde.

DELORES: Mr Chandler! You're supposed to have checked out hours ago. I got to make up this suite for the new guests.

CHANDLER: Oh sure kid! I'm all packed. I must have got lost in this story I'm writing. Gee it's tough. The studio says the audience don't want private dick films this year.

DELORES: (*Excitedly.*) Oh, are you using my idea? About the bunny rabbits going on a picnic?

CHANDLER: No kid, thanks for that tip but I don't think I could pull it off. No, horror is the big box office draw now.

DELORES: I really think you should give my idea a try. Everybody loves bunny rabbits. Anytime you get that writer's block again you come to me.

CHANDLER: You've been a doll. Listening to me gassing. I wish I could be more help with your problems.

DELORES: Oh but you have been. I went to see that shrink you recommended.

CHANDLER: Yeah?

DELORES: I felt like Claire Trevor in *Street of Chance.*

CHANDLER: Was he any help? Did he help you get your memory back?

DELORES: No, I still can't remember anything from before the cops found me by the freeway, except a bunch of movies I must have seen. But he did help me with the blackouts. And he's such a doll. 'Seems kinda troubled though. Like he's got the weight of the world on his shoulders. Like Dick Kiley in *Pick up on South Street.* Say! I know he works late. Maybe I'll give him a call and tell him how well I'm doing.

CHANDLER: Why don't you do that? Well, be seeing you kid. I hope you figure out where you come from and who you really are.

DELORES: Thank you Mr Chandler.

He exits.

I hope so too. I just don't feel I belong here in Angel City.

Mildred Pearce

AS I SAID TO MILDRED PEARCE
THIS ASPHALT JUNGLE GETS ME DOWN
FROM SUNSET BOULEVARD
OUT TO THE KEY
THEY SAY THAT MALTESE FALCONS
NEVER NEST AROUND CAPE FEAR
AND LIKE A LADY FROM SHANGHAI

I don't fit in round here.
(I'll)
Pick a cab up on South Street
I'm Central Station bound.
A Stranger on a Train
While the City Sleeps.
Life's DOA here
The Unsuspected's plain
I'm a Black Cat from Key Largo
Dodging Cross Fire in the rain.
The Gas Light's burning White Heat
And the Forest's Petrified
On Scarlet Street
They Live by Night and crime.
This Woman in the Window
Has no Shadow of a Doubt
She's become the Phantom Lady,
Bride of Frankenstein.
If I was tough as Garbo
Then I wouldn't give a damn.
But I'm the type of girl
Who needs to know just who I am.
Was life always like this?
If it was I don't recall
When girls like me
Didn't have to be
Some cheap Lauren Bacall.
I take a Big Sleep nowadays
And dream in black and white
Men with submachine guns
Jump from cars.
Indemnities are doubling
Caned Citizens hog the bar.
This broad is bored of
Shades of grey
And living in film noir.

She picks up the phone and dials.

Hello, could you connect me to Dr Edgar Harrington please? Hurry Honey. I'm at work and the hotel would fire me if they caught me using the telephone in the Victor Mature Suite (*Beat.*) Oh Dr Harrington, hi. It's Delores.

Dashing young DR EDGAR HARRINGTON is shown on the other end of the line.

EDGAR: Delores, my favourite patient. How are we today? No more of those memory blackouts I trust?

DELORES: No Dr, that's what I'm phoning to tell you. I still don't remember where I came from but I haven't been blacking out since you gave me those tablets and I feel as peppy as Liz Scott in *I Walk Alone.*

EDGAR: I'm glad to hear it. How many pills do you have left?

She reaches into her pocket and takes out a little bottle of pills.

DELORES: Just a moment.

She lays the receiver down by the side of the phone and pours pills into her hand to count them.

Lights down on EDGAR.
Maurice Critoph, the lecherous HOTEL MANAGER, enters. DELORES stands in front of the receiver so that he won't see that she's been using the phone.

HOTEL MANAGER: Ah Delores, there you are!

DELORES: Oh Mr Critoph, I was just about to change the sheets. Mr Chandler was a little late in checking out.

HOTEL MANAGER: I expect you were showing off those pretty legs of yours, you naughty, naughty girl.

DELORES: Certainly not Mr Critoph, and Mr Chandler is a perfect gentleman. I know he doesn't look at me that way.

HOTEL MANAGER: Skip it!

Tension underscoring.

All men look at you that way. You've bewitched us with your naughty, naughty peek-a-boo breasts and your 'I'm just a lost little girl' sighs and giggles. Well, I won't put up with it from a member of my hotel staff for a moment longer. I'm going to take you into that bedroom and give you the spanking you deserve, do you understand?

DELORES: But Mr Critoph, couldn't you just dock my pay like you do with everyone else you think looks at you funny?

HOTEL MANAGER: I think it's time I took a firm hand with you, my girl.

He starts to take off his jacket.
She backs off stage towards the bedroom with the MANAGER in pursuit.

DELORES: Oh Mr Critoph! No, really! Remember what happened to Jack Palance in *Sudden Fear*!

EDGAR still on the other end of the receiver.

EDGAR: Hello? Hello?

Back in the hotel room

DELORES: Mr Critoph! Please.

Underscoring out.

I haven't put little chocolates on the pillows yet!

Lights down on them.

Lights up on the EDITOR talking to his audience/reporters again.

EDITOR: Good news everybody, looks like we got a psycho killer! Word on the street is that last night's murder of (*He consults his notes.*) Mr Maurice Critoph, hotel manager at the Metropole, was a real humdinger. Who ever or what ever did this didn't just put a bullet through that bozo's brain, no they wrapped him up in some kind of web and sucked his innards out, just like a spider would. Thank God our cops are solving this with all their customary, speed, skill and finesse. This means they've got as much chance of catching this sicko as I have of making out with Shirley Temple! If this freak goes on a killing spree it could fill our pages for weeks to come. Lets cram tomorrow's edition so full of disgusting details we won't even have space for the crossword. I want you *Clarion* reporters all over that hotel like Errol Flynn in a nunnery.

Handsome cub reporter, JOE, emerges from the audience/ reporters. He is carrying some letters.

JOE: Excuse me, Sir! Last night at Delaney's I got talking to this bum 'works at the IRS. He says they're going through gangland tax returns like something's up. Should I investigate? I know it don't sound too interesting a story at the moment but I was thinking –

EDITOR: (*Hugging JOE and patting his cheek.*) You was thinking! You was thinking! I love this kid. Kid we don't employ you to think. We got grown reporters to do that, we got reporters so hard boiled, kiss their asses and you'd chip a tooth! So we don't need the mail room boy breaking into thought.

JOE: I'm not the mail room boy, sir. I edit the 'Lost and Found' column. You promoted me last summer.

EDITOR: I did? (*Beat.*) We got a 'Lost and Found' column?

JOE: Yes, sir at the back underneath the ads for hair tonic and male girdles.

EDITOR: (*Adjusting himself.*) Don't mock those girdles kid! (*Beat.*) Well, there you go, you got yourself a column, go write it and stop bugging me about the big boy's stuff.

JOE looks deflated.

Look, I'm not the kinda guy to stifle initiative and youthful ambition. Find me a cute human interest story – say a dame with big bazookas crying over a lost kitten – get down there with a camera and I might pull one of those fancypants theatre reviews and run your piece instead.

JOE: Oh gee thanks! But won't Mr DeMorbillon be upset… I mean his reviews...

EDITOR: He won't notice, kid. He only wakes up for the free booze at intermissions. Hey, stop grousing. I'm giving you a break ain't I?

JOE: I suppose so, sir, thank you.

EDITOR exits. JOE moves into his office.

(*To himself.*) This wasn't how they described things on the 'You too can win a Pulitzer Prize for journalism' correspondence course. A broom closet for an office that the cleaner always forgets is here, sharing with two hot water pipes and a spider's web that's been in that corner so long me and the owner are on first name terms. (*He looks up at the web on the fourth wall.*) Hey Harry, I'm talking to you! (*He looks at his sheath of letters.*) And the dumb letters I have to sift through. Where am I going to find a good story amongst this garbage?

He sings.

Lost and Found

'DEAR LOST AND FOUND
I'VE LOST MY CAT
I KNOW YOUR COLUMN OFTEN
DEALS WITH TRAGEDIES LIKE THAT.
HE'S NOT TOO SMART
A GINGER TOM,
I'VE HOLLERED FOR HIM
AND HIS COLLAR TELLS YOU
WHERE HE'S FROM.'

He puts down the letter and engages in a flight of fantasy.

OH RUN TIDDLES, RUN TIDDLES
GO ROB SOME STORES
GO ON A CRIME SPREE
GET BLOOD ON YOUR PAWS.
START A CAT MAFIA
FOR HEAVEN'S SAKE
A POSSE OF PUSSY'S
IS NEWS I COULD BREAK.

Picks up and reads out another letter.

'DEAR LOST AND FOUND
I'VE FOUND A DOG
HE WAS WANDERING BEWILDERED
IN THIS MORNING'S HEAVY FOG
I TOOK HIM IN
BUT HELP ME PLEASE
HE'S CHEWING UP THE CARPET
LEAVING DOGGY DO AND FLEAS.'

Another day dream.

OH KILL ROVER, WILL ROVER
YOU BRING ME FAME?
PLEASE COMMIT THE MURDER OF
THIS RUG LOVING DAME.

DON'T WASTE YOUR TIME
WITH YOUR FLEAS
AND YOUR POOP
A CRAZY DOG KILLER
COULD BE MY FIRST SCOOP.

Reading a third letter.

'Good money paid for mutated spiders. Specimens wanted for immediate experimentation. Apply in haste to the Arachnida Foundation, The Old Laboratory, Hillside, blah, blah, blah. Please note only persons with really hideously mutated specimens need apply.' (*He looks up at the web.*) Hey, Harry, you get any uglier and hairier and I'm taking you round to the lab sickos! (*Referring to the letter.*) Freaks.

He throws that letter away and picks up another.

Hey, what's this?

Light on DELORES.

DELORES: 'Dear Sir, I realise this is an unusual request but I've lost something. My past. You see the cops found me wandering on the freeway and I can't remember anything of who I am and how I got there. I just got a head full of old movies and an envelope in my pocket addressed to Delores, so I guess that's me, and the address of a bank. Nobody knew me there so I took a job at the Metropole Hotel across the street to see if anything jogs my memory, but so far nothing. Please could you ask if any of your readers knows who I am? Oh and when they found me I was carrying a suitcase of money. The nice policemen suggested I donate it to their Christmas fund, but if anybody wants the case back tell 'em to get in touch. It's real plastic.'

JOE: What a loony toon. Angel Town's like some weirdo magnet. No human interest here. Nothing even human.

DELORES: 'I enclose a picture in case it helps anyone recognise me'

Lights down on DELORES. JOE turns over the picture.

JOE: Holy Moses! Wow! Baby, baby, baby!

Sings.
So Joey, Go Joey
Run for the bus
A human interest
Tale with a plus.
Take your best note book
And cam'ra along

He picks up a camera.

She's human, I'm int'rested
What could go wrong?

Cross fade to JOE interviewing DELORES at the hotel. She's in her chambermaid's uniform as usual.

JOE: That's a very sad story, Miss…?

DELORES: Well that's just the thing, honey. I'm not sure what my second name is. All I could get from an envelope I found in my pocket was 'Miss Delores' and the rest had got ripped off when it was opened. But I've made up a name we could use.

JOE: Made up?

DELORES: Well I went to collect some pills, they asked for a second name and I thought 'this is dumb'. Everybody needs two names, right? So I just looked around me and chose the prettiest word in the drugstore.

JOE: So until we find out different you're Miss –?

DELORES: Laxilene. It's got a kind of a ring to it don't you think?

JOE: (*Also unaware.*) That's beautiful. What is it, French?

DELORES: I think it's Australian. The lady behind the counter looked a bit confused at my asking but she said it was something to do with 'down under'.

JOE: That's fascinating. Yep, you're a fascinating woman all right. In fact… I sure would like to get to know you a little better. I hope you don't think this is too forward but –

DELORES: You know, you're a sweet guy! Kinda like John Garfield in *Breaking Point.*

JOE: (*Flustered.*) Thanks I… I… if I could just take a few pictures.

JOE gets the camera ready.

DELORES: Well, please hurry I got to get back to work. We're understaffed since that horrible murder of Mr. Critoph last night. I wish I'd seen something 'could help the cops but I dropped all my pills and had one of my blackouts just before he died. They didn't seem too interested though. I guess it's just another dead guy to them. Angel City is a tough place isn't it?

JOE: Sure is. Now. Ready? Smile.

He takes a picture. The flash bulb goes off. DELORES screams.

DELORES: AGHHHHH!

JOE: What's the matter, honey?

DELORES: Nothing I… I… sorry I got some sort of a flash back. It was like… some kind of car headlights coming towards me. Oh don't you mind me. My dumb brain's all Barbara Stanwyck in *Sorry, Wrong Number.* Thanks for your time Mr –

JOE: Joe, my name's Joe Arnold. Here's *my* number just in case...you ever wanted to… see I was wondering if you and I could maybe, one night after you finish… What time do you get through?

DELORES: About ten thirty.

JOE: Jeez, they work you hard! No wonder you get blackouts.

DELORES: Oh, Dr Edgar gives me these great pills, they help a lot. (*Looks at watch.*) I really do have to go back to work now, thanks for putting me in the paper. (*Exit.*)

JOE: Well, you got my number in case you think of anything else!

But she's gone.

*An ornate telephone rings, lit by the light through a grand arch window. GRANGER, an imposing, unflappable english butler (*The Big Sleep*) answers the telephone.*

GRANGER: The DeLores mansion. I'm sorry Madame, Mr DeLores only takes calls from charlatans attempting to pass themselves off as his beautiful lost debutante daughter between the hours of ten and midday on Mondays and Thursdays. (*Beat.*) Yes, I dare say you *do* have the requisite identifying birth mark on your left buttock, so many of you do. My advise would be to give your self the doubtless rare experience of bathing and see whether is doesn't rub off with a little carbolic. In most cases we find that does the trick.

Beat – he holds the phone a little away from his ear as the person on the other line apparently screams some obscenity and then calmly, politely –

– and the same to you Madame. Do endeavour to have a nice day, won't you? (*He puts the phone down.*)

A grand door bell chimes. GRANGER goes off to answer it.

A beat then a weasely young man – IRWIN DeLORES – comes charging in followed by GRANGER.

IRWIN: Is the old man at home, Granger?

GRANGER: Yes Sir, and there's a young lady waiting to be interviewed for the position of your father's nurse.

IRWIN: What happened to fat old Miss Walker?

GRANGER: Alas, when your father's hands wandered a little too wantonly –

IRWIN: Miss Walker walked?

GRANGER: Waddled, Sir.

IRWIN: Not another one!

GRANGER: I suspect this new young lady may prove a match for him.

IRWIN: I haven't got time for all that nonsense. Get out.

GRANGER: Certainly, Sir

He exits.

IRWIN: Now, you old bastard, where do you keep your will?

He looks in likely places but is disturbed by a voice.

ESTELLA: Mr DeLores?

IRWIN: Yes?

IRWIN turns to find himself facing the devastatingly attractive nurse ESTELLA.

ESTELLA: I'm here for my interview.

IRWIN: Ah yes, I'm afraid you wouldn't do at all. You see… My father is very elderly with a very weak heart and too much stimulation could prove… (*Realising the advantage of her killing the old boy off.*) On second thoughts perhaps you might be just the thing. Well...um...an interview, yes. I see you keep yourself very... trim!

ESTELLA: I place a great deal of importance on regular physical exertion.

IRWIN: Even with the elderly?

ESTELLA: No one's allowed to slack when I'm in charge.

IRWIN: Very commendable I'm sure. Do tell me more –

ESTELLA: (*Sings.*)

Nurse Estella's Exercise Regime

NURSE ESTELLA'S EXERCISE REGIME
IF YOU FOLLOW IT
IT'S GONNA KEEP YOU
A HOT, FIT, LOVIN' MACHINE.
SO CLENCH 'EM TIGHT
THEN LET 'EM LOOSE
YOU'LL WORK UNTIL YOU SCREAM
NURSE ESTELLA'S EXERCISE REGIME.

JOHNNIE WEISSMULLER CAUGHT MY EYE.
WHAT A CAREER I PLANNED.
AND NOW HE'S TARZAN EVER SINCE
I TOOK HIS LOVE HANDLES IN HAND.
BETTY GRABLE, WHAT A STAR
THOSE LEGS, THAT SMILE, THAT BUST.
BUT THAT BABE WAS FLAT AS OLD LEMONADE
TILL I GOT HER TO SQUAT AND THRUST.

NURSE ESTELLA'S EXERCISE REGIME.
IF YOU FOLLOW IT
IT'S GONNA KEEP YOU
A HOT, FIT, LOVIN' MACHINE.
SO CLENCH 'EM TIGHT
THEN LET 'EM LOOSE
LET'S PUSH TO THE EXTREME
NURSE ESTELLA'S EXERCISE REGIME.

NO HUNK WOULD PLAY WITH POOR FAY WRAY
SHE CRAVED A HAIRY LOUT.
I GOT HER WORKING ON THAT TUSH
TILL A BIG APE ASKED HER OUT.
MICKEY ROONEY WAS UNFIT
FOR JUDY GARLAND'S CHARMS
SHE CALLED HIM MUNCHKIN TILL I CRUNCHED HIM
NOW THEY ARE BABES IN ARMS!

NURSE ESTELLA'S EXERCISE REGIME.
IF YOU FOLLOW IT
IT'S GONNA KEEP YOU
A HOT, FIT, LOVIN' MACHINE.
SO CLENCH 'EM TIGHT,
THEN LET 'EM LOOSE,
I THINK YOU GET THE THEME
NURSE ESTELLA'S EXERCISE REGIME.

NURSE ESTELLA'S EX -
NURSE ESTELLA'S EX -
NURSE ESTELLA'S EXERCISE REGIME.

IRWIN: Miss, I think your just what my frail, elderly, infirm father needs! Start immediately.

ESTELLA: Yes, Sir.

IRWIN fetches his decrepit father, OSWALD, wheeling him on in a chair at such an angle that the old man can't see ESTELLA yet. OSWALD has a copy of The Clarion *with him.*

OSWALD: Irwin, what the hell are you doing here?

IRWIN: Now Pappy, is that anyway to greet your only son?

OSWALD: Sure, when he's as big a creep as you.

IRWIN: And to think I've just engaged one of Angel City's top health care professionals to make your last few weeks on earth as happy, Pappy, as possible.

OSWALD: Sure, I bet she's as tough, ugly and cheap as the last few Medusas you sent me. Another day release from murderess row?

IRWIN wheels the chair round so that OSWALD sees ESTELLA.

OSWALD: Yowser!

ESTELLA: Would you like to see my particulars?

OSWALD clutches his heart.

OSWALD: How about you go prepare me a trial blanket bath and we'll take it from there.

ESTELLA: Yes, sir. (*She exits.*)

OSWALD: I'll be right up. (*Suspiciously.*) You must want something real bad?

IRWIN: Very well father, I'll cut to the chase. It's now six months since my so-called half-sister disappeared from that car wreck and I want to make sure you've finally cut her out of your will. I insist you come to your senses and face facts. (*Comforting.*) Poor little Sis died in that accident, Pappy, and keeping her in the will isn't going to bring her back now, is it?

OSWALD: You know they never found a body.

IRWIN: (*Hard again.*) Or the suitcase of money you asked her to deposit at the bank. Don't you think that little coincidence suggests the manipulative, celluloid-obsessed floozy has run off with the cash?

OSWALD: She would never steal from me, she was a wild child like her mother, but we always had more in common then you and I ever did.

IRWIN: Well, forgive me for not being the fruit of your squalid affair with a cheap Burlesque dancer rather then a loving marriage.

OSWALD: 'Loving!' As you well know, your late mother was about as lovable as a sack of scorpions! Her icy indifference to anything other then my bank balance drove me into the arms of Miss Fifi LaGrind. Did you really expect me to turn my back on our daughter when her mother was killed in that horrific industrial accident?

IRWIN: What exactly happened?

OSWALD: A python got a little too amorous during an exotic tableau in the Flatbush Follies of '31. My eyes still water thinking about it.

IRWIN: I did not expect you to take that brat in as an equal member of this family, with an equal share in your will.

OSWALD: You've that same glint in your eye your mother used to get when she mentioned money or drove the Pierce-Arrow over an endangered species.

IRWIN: Well, whether you like me or not I'm all the family you have left.

OSWALD: Perhaps not, you slimy streak of skunk deposit! Take a look at the this morning's paper.

He hands it over. IRWIN reads.

IRWIN: Where?

OSWALD indicates. IRWIN reads out.

'Name and claim this great dame.' Oh please! You're not seriously suggesting this nutty woman is lost little sister Anita?

OSWALD: Well, you got to admit it looks like her.

IRWIN: They all look like her, every single one of the harlots who's shown up since you announced Anita may have lost her memory in the car crash, and forgetten, tragically, she's entitled to half of a multimillion dollar inheritance! Can you imagine the line of peroxide wannabe beneficiaries stretching from here to Nebraska if you die without changing your will?

OSWALD: I think it's worth my meeting this young girl. She was found wandering on the freeway with half an envelope addressed to Miss DeLores and the address of the bank where I sent her.

IRWIN: So she says. They've all got some cock and bull story. Well I hope at least you won't object if I turn a private investigator on to this creature. See if I can get some juice from her past.

OSWALD: Son, you pick up dirt like tennis whites in an abattoir.

IRWIN: Well, you know what they say. 'Where there's a will, there's a feeding frenzy.'

Now we see JOE at a table with two coffees in front of him. DELORES arrives.

DELORES: Hi Joe, I'm so sorry I'm late. Thanks for saying you'd rush right over. The thing is I've got some wonderful, wonderful news. 'Cause of that story you wrote about me in this morning's paper I just got a telegram. This old guy, a Mr DeLores, wants to meet me at midnight tonight at his place, 88 Riverside Drive. He says he thinks he's my father.

JOE: Midnight?

DELORES: That's what I thought, but his nurse says the elderly have unusual sleep patterns. Oh won't it be wonderful to have a proper family again? Oh, oh wait. I got to telephone Dr Edgar with the good news. (*She takes her purse from her bag.*) I'm so happy. Just like Evelyn Keyes in *Johnny O'Clock*. Be right back – (*She goes.*)

Lights up on EDGAR reading the paper. He calls out to his receptionist.

EDGAR: (*To off.*) Nurse Emanuel, no more patients today. I'm exhausted. Except… if Delores comes by again, tell her to come right in.

He looks at her picture in the paper.

Oh Delores, you poor, poor angel. If only I had more confidence with women. Could you ever let me be more then just a highly qualified, trusted, medical professional? So I've got movie star looks, what use are they when I'm cursed with this gruesome existence? What girl would ever want to date a tall handsome Doctor?

Puts it down. Then picks it up and looks. Down again. Up. Down. Up.

Godammit! (*He sings.*)

About that Girl

CAN'T STOP THINKING ABOUT THAT GIRL
SHE DRIVES ME CRAZY
CAN'T STOP THINKING ABOUT THAT GIRL
AND THINKING MAYBE
SHE AND I WOULD LOOK SO GRAND
STEPPING OUT IN STYLE
HAND IN HAND AND
CAN'T STOP THINKING ABOUT THAT GIRL.

JOE sings.

JOE: CAN'T STOP DREAMIN' ABOUT THAT DOLL
GOIN' BANANAS
CAN'T STOP DREAMIN' ABOUT THAT DOLL
I WANNA PLAN US
MAYBE GOING DANCIN' SOMEWHERE
STEPPING OUT IN STYLE

STRUT BY STRUT BUT –
CAN'T STOP DREAMIN' ABOUT THAT DOLL.

DELORES returns.

DELORES: Aw, he gets kinda tongue tied. It's so sweet. Anyway I could tell he was pleased for me. So my daddy, what do you think he'll look like? I hope he'll be tall and kinda distinguished like Ralph Meeker in *Kiss Me Deadly* –

She continues talking in mute as lights take us to EDGAR, holding the phone as if he has just put down the phone to DELORES.

EDGAR: CAN'T HELP WOND'RIN ABOUT THAT GIRL
IS SHE THE ONE WHO –
CAN'T HELP WOND'RIN ABOUT THE GIRL –
NO! STOP AND RUN THROUGH
EVERYTHING YOU KNOW ABOUT HER –
DAMN I LOVE IT ALL!
BIT BY BIT IT –
KEEPS ME WOND'RIN ABOUT THAT GIRL.

Back to DELORES and JOE in the café. She hasn't stopped talking.

DELORES: – And so I was thinking if he likes seafood too maybe we could –

JOE: Whoa, whoa there honey. Look don't you think you should prepare yourself to be disappointed. I mean we don't know anything about this guy. What if he's some crank or somebody playing with you?

DELORES: Oh no. Nobody could be so mean. This is my pa alright. Hey maybe I've got brothers and sisters too. (*New thought.*) And if everybody liked sea food we could maybe get the family deal down at the crab shack next Sunday. I've always wondered what you get for the extra fifty cents.

JOE: All I'm saying is that maybe you shouldn't go alone tonight. It might not be safe?

DELORES: Oh Joe that's sweet of you but an attractive young amnesiac going alone to meet a mysterious stranger in a creepy old mansion at midnight? What could go wrong? We'll probably just be looking through old photograph albums and stuff. I tell you what though, maybe you could get a picture of us for the paper. You know, 'Father and daughter reunited'. This makes you look good too. Getting us together was a really swell thing to do. I could kiss you.

JOE: (*Not registering the kissing bit yet.*) Yeah, that's it. I'll come a long, just to record the happy event so then if there should happen to be any trouble… Midnight you say? 88 Riverside Drive?

DELORES: That's my daddy's address. And it's just along the freeway from where they found me!

JOE: Just a minute! About that kissing me thing –

DELORES: Oh my goodness look at the time. I got a get back to work. See you later hun.

She kisses him on the forehead and rushes out.

JOE: I'm never gunna wash again. (*Sings.*)

CAN'T STOP BEAMIN' ABOUT THAT BROAD
SHE'S SOMETHIN' ELSE, 'CAUSE –

JOE AND EDGAR:
CAN'T STOP DREAMIN' ABOUT THAT GIRL.

EDGAR:
SHE'S GOT ME JEALOUS

BOTH:
IF I COULD BE THE GUY FOR HER

I'D SHOUT IF FROM THE ROOF
CRY, SKY HIGH. I

EDGAR: CAN'T STOP MY STRESSIN' ABOUT THAT –

JOE: THIS GUY'S OBSESSIN' ABOUT THAT –

BOTH: WON'T STOP GUESSIN' ABOUT THAT

JOE: DAME

EDGAR: LADY

JOE: BROAD

EDGAR: ANGEL

JOE: CUTIE PIE

EDGAR: PATIENT

BOTH: GIRL!

Blackout.

In the darkness we hear the majestic doorbell of the DeLores residence. No answer. And again.
Then the gothic sound of a huge door creaking open.
Tension underscoring.
We see JOE walking tentatively into the mansion. He has his camera.

JOE: Hello! Hello! Anybody home? (*To himself.*) Gee look at this place, what is it, early Addams Family? (*Out loud.*) Hello, the door was open. Hope you don't mind me coming right in. I believe I'm expected. Joe Arnold, from the *Clarion* newspaper. Delores? Mr DeLores? (*He twigs the connection.*) Hey! That fits! Delores, DeLores. Why didn't I think of that?

He spots OSWALD in his wheel chair with his back to us.

Hello? Mr DeLores?

He walks to the front of the wheel chair and screams in horror at what he sees.

Aghhhhhh!

GRANGER the butler appears behind him. He turns, sees GRANGER and screams again.

JOE: Aghhhhhh!

GRANGER: (*Deliberately misquoting the Cole Porter.*) 'Mr DeLores regrets he's unable to lunch today, Madame.' Sorry, I've always wanted to say that.

JOE: Did you… Did you…do this?

GRANGER: Entwine Old Mr DeLores in a sticky web and devour him until nothing remains but a pulpy mess of bloody, bone, tissue and half-digested internal organs? No sir. I found the master very much as we see him now on my return from a half day visiting Mother. Alas she's been a little poorly of late but nothing serious I'm happy to report. (*Beat.*) As my wages are fully paid until the end of the week might I offer you some refreshment?

JOE: Shouldn't we…shouldn't we…? I mean…we should call the cops?

GRANGER: The police are on their way, Sir.

JOE: Wait, was there a girl here, a beautiful blonde girl, looking for her father?

GRANGER: Whilst I was on my half day off? I couldn't possibly say, Sir. Mr DeLores Junior did drop in ten minutes before you arrived though, Sir and left in a somewhat excitable state.

JOE looks at the mess in the wheel chair and nearly throws up.

JOE: I got to get out of here.

He faints.
Nurse ESTELLA enters in coat with suitcase.
GRANGER looks down at JOE.

GRANGER: Forgive me, Miss. I do believe you've some kind of nursing qualification I wonder if you'd be so kind as to assist me in resuscitating this young gentleman?

ESTELLA: You're kidding, right?

GRANGER: I'm not one of life's great kidders, Miss.

ESTELLA: I'm out of here. What's there to stick around for? There's no one to pay our wages.

GRANGER: Very true Miss, and yet –

ESTELLA: And yet nothing! As my darling Mother said when she walked out on us on Christmas morning with my father's fortune under one arm and the turkey under the other –

She sings.

Adios!

ESTELLA:
YOU' GOTTA KNOW WHEN TO QUIT
WHEN TO HEAD FOR THE DOOR
YOU SHOULD ALWAYS BOW OUT
WHILE THEY'RE SCREAMING FOR MORE.
NEVER WATCH FROM THE WINGS
IF IT ISN'T YOUR SCENE
FIX YOUR EYES STRAIGHT AHEAD
WHO CARES WHERE YOU'VE BEEN!

GRANGER tries to convince himself she's right.

GRANGER: (*Spoken.*) Yes! Yes!
(*Sings.*) RIGHT, I'LL CANCEL THE MILK
SHOULD I LEAVE AN ADDRESS?

'THINK I'LL LOWER THE BLINDS
'CAUSE THE CARPET'S A MESS!
I'LL JUST FLICK ROUND FOR DUST
MAYBE PLUMP THE POUFFE (*Two syllables.*)
I'VE GOT ONE OF MY HEADS
P'RHAPS I'D BETTER STAY.

Call and response sequence. GRANGER slightly overlapping.

ESTELLA: LEARN TO SAY 'ADIOS'
GRANGER: SHOULD I PACK FOR THE SUN?
ESTELLA: AND FORGET AU REVOIR
GRANGER: OR JUST TAKE WINTER CLOTHES?
ESTELLA: IF YOU'RE STUCK IN THE MUD
GRANGER: WILL MY PASSPORT EXPIRE?
ESTELLA: YOU WON'T GET VERY FAR
GRANGER: I'VE A SNIFFILY NOSE!
ESTELLA: TRY TO KICK UP SOME DUST
GRANGER: BUT YOU'VE MADE A GOOD CASE
ESTELLA: GOTTA COVER SOME GROUND.
GRANGER: I SUPPOSE I CAN SEE
ESTELLA: KISS, KISS IT'S BEEN GREAT
GRANGER: THERE'S NO REASON TO STAY
ESTELLA: BUT I'LL SEE YOU AROUND.
GRANGER: WHERE THERE'S NOTHING FOR ME,
GRANGER: (*Spoken.*) I say, would you care to dance?
ESTELLA: (*Spoken.*) What's to stop us?

Soft shoe verse
Then

BOTH: YOU' GOTTA KNOW WHEN TO QUIT
WHEN TO HEAD FOR THE DOOR
YOU SHOULD ALWAYS BOW OUT
WHILE THEY'RE SCREAMING FOR MORE.
NEVER WATCH FROM THE WINGS
IF IT ISN'T YOUR SCENE
FIX YOUR EYES STRAIGHT AHEAD
WHO CARES WHERE YOU'VE BEEN.

Key change.
GRANGER gets rather carried away and tries some Gospel jammin'.

ESTELLA: LEARN TO SAY ADIOS
GRANGER: ADIOS BABY!
ESTELLA: AND FORGET AU REVOIR
GRANGER: OH NO AU REVOIRS!
ESTELLA: IF YOU'RE STUCK IN THE MUD
GRANGER: DON'T STICK IT!
BOTH: (*In harmony.*) YOU WON'T GET VERY FAR
ESTELLA: TRY TO KICK UP SOME DUST
GRANGER: KICK YOUR HEELS UP MUMMA!
ESTELLA: GOTTA COVER SOME GROUND
GRANGER: GOT IT COVERED, CUSTER!
ESTELLA: KISS, KISS IT'S BEEN GREAT
GRANGER: (*Two air kisses.*) MOI! MOI!

BOTH: BUT I'LL SEE YOU AROUND.
KISS, KISS IT'S BEEN GREAT
BUT I'LL SEE YOU AROUND.

The sound of a humbler door bell ringing. No answer, ringing again. Lights up on DELORES' apartment.

DELORES: OK, OK, I'm coming. My head feels like Edmond O'Brien's in *DOA*.

She staggers to the door in a state of much disarray and lets in IRWIN who bursts through dramatically.

IRWIN: So I've finally tracked you to your web, little Miss Muffet! (*But then he practically collapses panting from exhaustion.*) Jesus! It's a lot of stairs to get up here.

DELORES: Do I know you? Sorry my head's not too clear I get these blackouts you see and I've just come round from a nasty one. You wouldn't happen to be a door to door aspirin seller would you?

IRWIN: Oh yes. The famous memory blackouts, Miss? Are you intending to keep up this masquerade as Anita DeLores this evening? (*Suddenly struck by –*) You sure do look like her. I got to admit that. Nice job.

DELORES: It's Laxilene actually. Miss Delores Laxilene. And you are?

IRWIN: Mr Irwin DeLores.

DELORES: Mr DeLores! Daddy? You're a lot younger then I expected. Hey, maybe that makes me a lot younger then I expected!

IRWIN: I believe your appointment tonight was with my father.

DELORES: But that means – I'm your little sister!

IRWIN: Oh drop it!

DELORES: My! Look at the time, Junior. I was supposed to be at Daddy's house on Riverside Drive hours ago! I came home after work to smarten up and –

IRWIN: – And you had one of your convenient blackouts. Just like you told the police you had before entangling the hotel manager of the Metropole in a web and sucking his body into a bloody pulp. Exactly the same treatment you gave my father this evening.

DELORES: Could you go a little slower Bro? I got a nasty old headache.

IRWIN: Have you sweetie? Well let's see if I can't break things down a little simpler for you. I believe you murdered my father tonight just the same as you murdered that hotel manager. And claiming a memory blackout isn't going to cut it with me I'm afraid.

DELORES: Just a minute – Daddy's dead? But I only just found him.

IRWIN: Oh spare me the dramatics. If he *had* been your father you'd remember he was an evil old bastard, memory loss or no memory loss. And you'd be as indifferent to his passing as I am. The only thing that matters to you and I is his will and your despicable attempts to pass yourself off as his daughter in order to claim half of it.

DELORES: What are you saying? I don't want anything from daddy except a father's love, and well maybe a pony if he's as rich as you say.

IRWIN: Very convincing but save it for the jury when they try you for his gruesome murder.

DELORES: But I'd never murder anybody.

IRWIN: Oh yeah that's right you'd be too busy having a memory blackout. Listen lady, I've had you investigated by the sharpest private eye in the business and I got some pretty interesting dirt on you, like from the investigating officer on the Critoph case, oh, and that receptionist at the shrink's office where your boyfriend works.

DELORES: Dr Edgar is not my boyfriend – though a girl can dream.

IRWIN: You, Miss, are a psychopath with a twisted penchant for killing as a spider. Well I was one step ahead of you! Thanks for getting rid of my father but you're not going to see one penny of that inheritance.

DELORES: I wouldn't want something that wasn't mine. Did Daddy ever mention me? Do you think he loved me? You'll stay with me though won't you bro? Say, do you like sea food? Don't leave me all alone like Ida Lupino in *High Sierra.*

IRWIN: I'm going to do you a deal. (*He takes a document from his jacket pocket.*) Sign this affidavit dropping all claims to my father's money and I won't tell the police you're a killer.

DELORES: This is all too confusing – I'm scared I might have one of my blackouts.

IRWIN: There are no blackouts! You're a cold blooded murderess! But once you sign this paper that'll be nobody's business but your own.

He hands over the paper.
She attempts to read it.

DELORES: Could I take a moment to look this through, Bro? I'm still a little confused about my new family.

IRWIN: Really? Well, you play dumb as long as you like, Honey. I ain't going nowhere until I've secured my father's inheritance. After twenty-five years of playing the dutiful son, I reckoned I've earned it.

DELORES: Could you help me here?

IRWIN: Sure, I think you'll find it's legally binding.

DELORES: When it says 'I the undersigned', does that mean I have to stand under some kind of a sign?

IRWIN: Jeez!

DELORES: (*A realisation.*) Say! You're not my brother at all!

IRWIN: At last!

DELORES: You're one of those pushy, unscrupulous encyclopaedia salesmen ain't yah? I read you guys never leave 'till you got the householder signed up for all thirty six books. One for each letter of the alphabet.

IRWIN: JUST SIGN THE PAPER YOU MESSED UP BROAD! YOU'RE GIVING ME A MIGRAINE!

DELORES: Oooh, maybe old Mrs Granger next door has some aspirin. Would you like me to go wake her? I sure could use one too.

IRWIN: Not so fast, d'you think I was born yesterday? You ain't going nowhere till you sign on the dotted line.

DELORES: (*She reads.*) Look, I was right! Encyclopaedias – 'Clause A, Clause B, Clause C'. Funny, then it skips to 'D'.

IRWIN: (*Grasps his head.*) ALRIGHT! GET SOME ASPIRIN! But don't try anything smart or I'm straight out of here and round to the police.

DELORES exits. A rumble of thunder.

So Pappy, what d'you think of your only son now? Thought I was such a sap, eh? Well just you watch me take this city. See me scoop it up in my arms like some beautiful babe and then hear it scream for mercy as I nail it to the floor. No more black and white. It's time for the little guy to start living in Technicolor and you're pickin' up the tab, every last cent, Daddy Dearest.

There's a slow menacing knock at the door.
Tension underscoring.

Well, you got the key.

More knocking.

Hey, what you trying to pull? I told you, don't get smart. Not if you wanna keep the cops out of this.

Now scrabbling from behind the door.

Blondie is that you?

More scrabbling.

Silence.
Then more knocking.
IRWIN takes a gun from his pocket then cautiously opens the door.
The door opens inwards at such an angle that the audience can not see who's behind it. But IRWIN can.

Oh my God! AGHHHHH!

He can't bear to look at what ver it is. He fires the gun repeatedly in quick succession.
But it seems to have no effect on the unseen visitor. He attempts to fire again and again but the gun doesn't go off anymore – empty.
IRWIN backs away from the visitor's apparent advance. He falls to his knees.

Please, please don't hurt me. I'll do anything.
SOMEBODY HELP ME. PLEASE!

Blackout.

End of Act One.

ACT TWO

A bloody IRWIN is hanging upside down in a spider's web, staring at his assailant.

IRWIN: Oh my God! From what fiery pit of hell did you emerge, you half-human, half-spider freak? Why are you licking your lips at me like that? Don't eat me, I beg of you. Oh God, what a terrible end.

B Picture Acting

(*Operatic.*) No! No! No!
I pray to the all-powerful gods
Of Samuel Goldwyn and Louis B Meyer
Spare me from meeting a terrible end
At the eight sticky feet
Of this great spider slayer.
Spare me this horrible fate
Each part I've played's
Had a death scene to date.
Oh why can't my agent get me a deal
Where I get to live to the final reel –

Lights change destroying the horror atmosphere.

For once I'd love to be the leading actor
Not the creepy guy who ends up dead,
Just one time to get a blaze of glory
Not this gory end or with a belly full of lead.

B picture acting is a crazy way to earn.
'Wish I could do something more profound.
Three whole years at the method acting studio
Just to be a bozo RKO can kick around.
Thought I'd soon progress beyond film noirs
Cameos for studios with only two-bit stars,
But they tell me, audiences flock
And it pays better then Chekhov

THOUGH THE SCRIPT IS TOTAL SCHLOCK!

The OSWALD DeLORES actor enters.

OSWALD: I don't know what you've got to complain about. At least you got a decent death scene. As the old father I had to meet my maker facing the wall in a wheel chair. No close ups, nothing! When I think of my Off-Broadway work...

I PLAYED THE BARD THE CRITICS WERE ENRAPTURED.
MY HAMLET WAS THE BEST OF '29
HOLLYWOOD, THEY SAID MUST SURLY BECKON
BECKONED? BOY, I'M LUCKY IF I GET ONE DECENT LINE.

BOTH:
B PICTURE ACTING IS A CRAZY WAY TO EARN.
'WISH WE COULD DO SOMETHING MORE PROFOUND.
THREE WHOLE YEARS AT THE METHOD ACTING STUDIO
JUST TO BE THE BOZOS RKO CAN KICK AROUND.
THOUGHT WE'D SOON PROGRESS BEYOND FILM NOIRS
CAMEOS FOR STUDIOS WITH ONLY TWO-BIT STARS,
SAME OLD CARDBOARD CHARACTERS TO PLAY
WE'RE PROPS WITH A HEARTBEAT,
YET WE SHOW UP HERE EV'RY DAY.

The HOTEL MANAGER actor appears.

HOTEL MANAGER: You two got it lucky. My agent got me the part of the lecherous hotel manager. I told her – I'm romantic lead material. My analyst said this could be doing me permanent damage.

IRWIN: (*Sings.*)
MY WIFE SAYS I'M A CERT FOR BIBLE EPICS.

HOTEL MANAGER:
I SHOULD BE PLAYING COSTUME DRAMA ROLES.

OSWALD:
NEXT WEEK THEY GOT ME PLAYING TONTO'S FATHER!

IRWIN:

YOU'RE LUCKY! I'LL BE STOOD WHILE GANGSTERS SHOOT ME FULL OF HOLES.

ALL:

B PICTURE ACTING IS A CRAZY WAY TO EARN.
'WISH WE COULD DO SOMETHING MORE PROFOUND.
THREE WHOLE YEARS AT THE METHOD ACTING STUDIO
JUST TO BE THE BOZOS RKO CAN KICK AROUND.
THOUGHT WE'D SOON PROGRESS BEYOND FILM NOIRS
CAMEOS FOR STUDIOS WITH ONLY TWO-BIT STARS,
BUT THERE'S ALWAYS FEMME FATALES TO FIGHT
IF ONLY LIFE COULD BE THIS FUN
AND JUST AS BLACK AND WHITE.

STUDIO FLOOR MANAGER'S VOICE: (*Off.*) OK, OK, back to work.

Everyone but IRWIN clears the set.

Studio bell rings.

VOICE: (*Off.*) Lights, Camera, action!

Music and lights take us back into the world of Femme Fatale.

IRWIN: No. No I beg of you. Show some mercy please!

Blackout.
In the darkness the sound of IRWIN's screams as he's eaten by a human spider.
Spider belch!

Lights up on DELORES furiously banging on an apartment door.

DELORES: Mrs Granger, Mrs Granger – it's Delores. From across the hall. You got to let me use your phone. Something terrible's happened!

The door opens to reveal GRANGER the butler, as unflappable as ever.

GRANGER: Yes, Madame? Can I help you?

DELORES: Mrs Granger has a butler now? Last week she was on welfare!

GRANGER: Alas mother has seen no upturn in her financial circumstances, something which we've every confidence will change when my compensation comes through.

DELORES: Look, honey can I just use your phone? I'll pay yah, it's just that it's an emergency. I had a another blackout, I came to, there was a bullet holes in the wall and when I opened my apartment door – Oh! It's too horrible.

GRANGER; Might I be so bold as to enquire whether you are referring to the discovery of decomposing human remains suspended in a gigantic spider's web?

DELORES: How did you know?

GRANGER: Won't you come in, Miss –

DELORES: Laxi – please call me Delores. The phone? May I please?

GRANGER: I wouldn't trouble yourself, Madame. My instinct, too, was to dial the authorities, when I found the half eaten remains of my employer. But, as an officer will tell you, they turn something of a blind eye to such occurrences.

DELORES: (*Suspiciously.*) Maybe I wasn't planning to call the cops.

GRANGER; It's not that they're uncaring. In fact quite the opposite. They hush these things up as much as possible because those shocked at finding the bodies tend to prefer things that way. You see it means they'll be offered compensation.

DELORES: Could I please just use your –

GRANGER: Someone from a secret organisation known as the Arachnida Foundation will be in touch to offer you a very generous sum of money in return for overlooking your unpleasant discovery.

Lights and music make the following innocent line from DELORES seem ominous.

DELORES: Say, you know a lot don't you mister? You wanna be careful. It can be dangerous knowing too much in Angel City. Remember poor Ed Cornell in *I Wake Up Screaming*?

Back to normal. GRANGER didn't notice.

GRANGER: I must say their hygiene operatives do make an excellent job of cleaning up the evidence. There's an awful lot of grateful people out there, Miss. I'm sure you wouldn't want to be the first person to rock the boat.

The Compensation Quadrille

GRANGER:

I'VE ALWAYS BEEN A BUTLER TO
THE RICH AND THE ELITE.
I POLISHED UP THEIR EGOS,
BLEW THEIR NOSES, WIPED THEIR FEET.
ALTHOUGH I'M AWFULLY SORRY
THAT SUCH SLAUGHTER'S COME TO PASS
THE COMPENSATION MEANS
I NEEDN'T KISS ANOTHER ARSE.

GRATEFUL CITIZENS:

AH, AH. AH, AH. KISS ANOTHER ASS.

CITIZEN:

I always dreamed of sunset skies
And cocktails on the beach
But whilst I lived with Eunice
Such a life was out of reach.
No one likes to find their spouse
A pulpy bloody ball
But since the compensation came
I don't miss her at all.

GRATEFUL CITIZENS:

Ah, ah. Ah, ah. Don't miss her at all.

CITIZEN:

Dear Grandpa was a tiresome man
When in a grumpy mood.
But on the whole I was upset
To find him spider food.
The cheque helped to remind me
Of the charms which grandpa lacked
And now I've many relatives
I wish the thing'd attack.

GRATEFUL CITIZENS:

Ah, ah. Ah, ah. Wish the thing'd attack.

FEMALE CITIZEN:

My husband was a brilliant man,
I always heard it said,
Brilliant business, brilliant sportsman
Brilliant guy to wed.
I found his brilliant body pulped,
A psycho'd been at work
Then money helped me realise
He'd always been a jerk.

GRATEFUL CITIZENS:

Ah, ah. Ah, ah. Always been a jerk.
And many other citizens

ARE GRATEFUL AT THIS TIME
AND ALL HAVE FOUND THEIR HAPPINESS
THROUGH GHASTLY BRUTAL CRIME.
A MOST UNLIKELY SAVIOUR CAME
WHEN EVERYTHING SEEMED BLEAK
A PSYCHOPATHIC, FLESH DEVOURING
HALF-MAN, SPIDER FREAK.

JOE is now with DELORES, both with letters.

DELORES: You got a letter from the Arachnida Foundation too?

JOE: Yep, a few hours after I found the old guy's mutilated body. They're hushing up anyone who sees the monster's victims.

DELORES: Well, I guess that's a kinda nice thing to do. Give people a new start.

JOE: It's really weird.

DELORES: They offered you a lot of dough, right?

He hands her a letter. She reads.

'In light of the considerable distress discovering this corpse must have… blah, blah… the Arachnida Foundation would like to offer you a sum of –'
Me too! We're rich! Oh Joe, now you can give up your crumby job at the paper.

JOE: Honey bun! You don't think I accepted do you?

DELORES: You didn't?

JOE: No. This is an international scandal. People are being murdered in the most gruesome, heartless way and no one's doing anything about it. I just can't take their blood money. I just can't. (*Beat.*) And what's more this story could get me promoted and even win me a Pulitzer Prize!

DELORES: Wow! It's nice to win a prize. What do you get?

JOE: Umm, I'm not sure.

DELORES: Henry on reception, his mom won a set of steak knives in a competition once. (*Excited at the prospect.*) Could your prize be steak knives?

JOE: Maybe!

DELORES: Wow!

JOE: Well, I gotta get the scoop first. Who are these Arachnida Foundation people? There's just a bank address on these letters and they're not listed anywhere. If we knew where they were I could go search for clues.

DELORES: Joe, you be careful. We don't want you ending up as spider food or who's going to claim your prize?

JOE: 'Arachnida', 'Arachnida', that sure rings a bell. Where have I heard that name before? –

DELORES: You'll figure it out. I got real faith in you.

JOE: Me? Nobody's ever had faith in me before.

DELORES: Can I call you when I finish work? I want to know what you found out. (*Suspiciously.*) Just in case.

JOE: 'Just in case' what?

DELORES: Oh nothing.

JOE: Honey don't call me, we can do better then that. Why don't you meet me at Petruchio's?

DELORES: The romantic little Italian place on the corner of 5th?

JOE: (*Trying to be cool.*) Is it romantic? I never thought of it that way.

DELORES: Joe?

JOE: Yeah.

DELORES: Would you like it to be? Romantic, I mean?

JOE: Yeah, yeah I guess that would be kinda nice!

DELORES: I'll see you after work, then.

JOE: Sure thing, kitten.

DELORES: (*Sudden panic.*) Oh but Joe, you will show up won't you? I don't want to be like poor Barbara Stanwyck sat all alone in that creepy joint waiting for Wendell Corey.

JOE: Honey! Honey! I'm gonna be there. The truth is I'm nuts about yah.

DELORES: Oh Joe, I don't know what I'd do without you and Dr Edgar. I'd be all alone in the world.

JOE: Well, you won't be alone at Petruchio's tonight.

DELORES: Promise?

JOE: Cross my heart.

He sweeps her up in a Hollywood kiss.

See you later gorgeous. (*He exits.*)

Lights and music suddenly once again make DELORES appear sinister.

DELORES: You'd better show mister, or I'll get real angry, and I'm not so pretty when I'm angry!

DELORES exits.

JOE is in his Lost and Found office again.

JOE: (*Musing, looks around.*) Gee! Why does that cleaner always forget to do my office? Look at the size of Harry's web now. Hey, you're turning into a real monster, mister. You ain't gonna be winning any beauty contests. How much hair you sprouting there, fellah? Arachnida!

JOE suddenly remembers something. He goes scrabbling in the waste paper basket and pulls a paper out.

Here it is. Here it is! This is it! I knew I'd heard that name before (*He reads.*) 'Good money paid for mutated spiders. Specimens wanted for immediate experimentation. Apply in haste to the *Arachnida* Foundation, The Old Laboratory –' and there's an address just out of town! (*Looks at web and opens a match box from his pocket.*) Harry! Oh Harry! You and I are going for a little trip to the country.

A grand room at the Arachnida Foundation.
MAXWELL, an enormously fat lawyer, addresses the audience.

MAXWELL: Welcome friends of Arachnida –

To MAXWELL's irritation JOE comes in late and sits amongst the audience.

JOE: Sorry, I'm late, sorry (etc).

MAXWELL begins again.

MAXWELL: Welcome friends of Arachnida – and interested parties in the estate of Oswald DeLores. I know some of you are wondering why the late Mr DeLores' last will and testament is to be read out here at the Arachnida foundation. All will become clear in a few moments. So let us not waste anymore time. Time is money. (*Amused.*) Particularly my time. (*He opens his briefcase to retrieve the will.*)

JOE leans over to a member of the audience.

JOE: He ain't kiddin either. That's Maxwell Bullock. The original fat-cat lawyer. They say he charges two Gs an hour. He's got to be worth as much as old DeLores himself.

MAXWELL: (*Opens an envelope.*) And the winner is.... Just my little joke there. Due to the shocking, sudden and unexpected demise of Mr Irwin DeLores, Mr Oswald DeLores' only son, the entire estate divides into two. Firstly I am authorised to inform you that in recognition of her profound impact on Mr Oakley Senior's final days he bequeaths fifty per cent of his fortune to his last nurse (*Indicating her.*) Ms Estella Harrington.

Gasps.

Estella. Won't you join us?

Sexy sax underscoring. ESTELLA enters, dressed in mourning, looking Lauren Bacall stunning.
MAXWELL kisses ESTELLA's hand.

Further. As I've been unable to trace Miss Anita DeLores, Oswald's missing step-daughter, his will now states that the remaining fifty per cent of the fortune should be donated to a charity of Ms Harrington's choosing.

ESTELLA: I am delighted to announce that I have chosen to donate this substantial sum to the Arachnida Foundation for their continued research into spider mutations.

MAXWELL: On behalf of deformed bugs everywhere, thank you.

JOE: Just a minute I have a question. Joe Arnold – *The Clarion.* Based on mug shots, I got reason to believe that this broad is also known as the Black Widow, on the run from justice in five states for grabbing rich, ailing millionaires by their will and testaments. Got anything to say, lady?

MAXWELL: That is complete fabrication, young man. I can assure you there's absolutely nothing untoward about this gorgeous, generous-lipped, taut yet silky-skinned, fine, upstanding example of American womanhood.

JOE: Then maybe she's got her hooks into you too?

MAXWELL: How dare you! Security, throw this damn fool out.

ESTELLA: Maxwell, let me handle this. I'm sure I can clear up any confusion. Young stallions like our friend here always assume that if a beautiful woman is attracted to a mature man like you she must be after his money. Well, not me.

MAXWELL: Of course not, my darling.

ESTELLA: (*To the band.*) Hit it!

She sings.

Just an Unusual Girl

SOME DAMES NEVER DEIGN TO SAMPLE
FAT, OLD MEN, FOR AN EXAMPLE.
BUT I LIKE 'EM GREY AND AMPLE
I'M JUST AN UNUSUAL GIRL.
YOUTH'S AN OVERRATED QUALITY
I MUCH PREFER MATURITY
A FELLAH WITH A FRAME THAT'S CUDD-A-LY
GEE HE'S FOR ME!

MAX:
SHE'S JUST AN UNUSUAL GIRL!

ESTELLA:
WHILE OTHER DOLLS SEEK OUT A HUNKY MATE
I'M CHUBBY-CHASING CHUMS WITH EXCESS WEIGHT
KEEP YOUR CARY GRANTS AND YOUR FRED ASTAIRES
MY TASTE'S FOR THE FULLER WAISTLINES
OF OLD MILLIONAIRES.
SOME FOLK CLAIM I'M ONLY DIGGING GOLD

I WISH THE CYNICS WOULDN'T SCOLD
JUST 'CAUSE I LIKE 'EM RICH AND OLD
I'M JUST AN UNUSUAL GIRL.
I JUST LOVE TO ROLL AROUND BENEATH
A GUY WHO HASN'T HIS OWN TEETH
I FIND TO TOUCH A TOUPEE TURNS ME WEAK
BUT I'M NO FREAK

MAX:
SHE'S JUST AN UNUSUAL GIRL!

ESTELLA:
HERE'S A MESSAGE FOR YOU MILLIONAIRES
DO YOU GET OUT OF BREATH JUST CLIMBING STAIRS?
IF YOU'RE SPROUTING HAIR FROM EITHER EARS OR NOSE
I WILL SET YOUR HEART A POUNDING
TILL THAT BABY GOES –
BUMPITY, BUMPITY, BUMPITY
BUMPITY, BUMPITY, BUMPITY
BUMPITY, BUMPITY, BUMPITY
BUMPITY, BUMPITY, BUMPITY
BUMPITY, BUMPITY, POW!

MAX:
SOME DAMES NEVER DEIGN TO SAMPLE
FAT, OLD MEN, FOR AN EXAMPLE.
BUT SHE LIKES 'EM GREY AND AMPLE

ESTELLA:
I'M JUST AN UNUSUAL GIRL.

MAX:
YOUTH'S AN OVERRATED QUALITY
SHE MUCH PREFERS MATURITY
A FELLAH WITH A FRAME THAT'S CUDD-A-LY

ESTELLA:
GEE HE'S FOR ME!
I'M AN UNUSUAL

MAX:

SHE'S AN UNUSUAL

BOTH:

JUST AN UNUSUAL GIRL!

ESTELLA:

COME ON GRANDPA – GIVE ME A WHIRL!

JOE: Well, she might fool you mister but she don't fool me! She's the Black Widow alright and what's more the Arachnida Foundation here is sheltering a half-human, half-spider, serial-killer freak.

ESTELLA: That's enough! I think we've been very patient. You're on private property. (*Calls.*) Manfred, Axel, Lock him up until I decide what to do with him. (*Exits.*)

Two thugs in white coats and lab goggles enter and take JOE from the auditorium at gun point.

JOE: Hey, No! Hey! look you can't lock me up – you see I got a date tonight. I promised! If I don't show up she'll think I'm a heel.

Meanwhile DELORES is crossing her hotel lobby carrying a big gothic bunch of orchids and singing to herself.

DELORES: 'Can't stop thinking about my guy.' (*Calls to off.*) Miss Farrell, would you like me to take these flowers up to the guest's room?

(*To herself.*) Hey, they're like the ones that old guy grows in *The Big Sleep*? What number are they for?

She looks at the card.

Oh! Oh! They're addressed to me. Oh Joe, you angel. You shouldn't have. I can't wait to see you tonight.

She rips open the envelope.

(*Sings.*) 'Can't stop dreamin' about my prince.' (*She glances at the letter.*) Oh! Oh! Oh my goodness!

EDGAR appears in a spot light. Romantic underscoring.

EDGAR: My dear Delores, please accept these flowers as a token of my feelings for you. Ever since you first walked into my life, I've done nothing but think of you. From our sessions I feel I know you so well and yet there's so much I don't know about you. Please give me a chance to experience your smile in the winter sunshine, to recognise your laugh across a crowded restaurant, to catch perhaps a look of affection in your beautiful eyes. Please tell me you could come to care for me as I care for you. Forgive my writing this rather then telling you face to face but the fear of your rejection turns me to ice. Yours always, E.

Music out. Back to DELORES.

DELORES: (*Moved.*) Aww! (*But then.*) Who's E? Oh! But I've given my heart to Joe. Poor Dr Edgar! Maybe if he'd asked me to be his girl first.... Now I know why Jan Sterling looks so confused in *Appointment with Danger.* Well, when Joe walks through that door tonight I guess I'll know in my heart whether he's the right guy for me. (*Beat.*) Or whether I should run to Dr Edgar. (*She exits.*)

Back to MAXWELL and ESTELLA at the Arachnida Foundation, post will.

MAXWELL: (*In the direction of JOE's exit.*) And I'm phoning your Editor to have you fired. (*Charming, to his audience.*) I think we're just about through now, friends. And what a fitting tribute to dear departed Oswald's memory that some of his hard earned money will bring hope to the mutated spiders of America.

ESTELLA: (*Spotting VIPs.*) Mrs Rockefeller! Miss Vanderbilt! I'm so glad you could join us. I wonder if I might trouble you for a little donation towards the foundation's work.

MAXWELL: Everyone! There's a book of condolence on the way out if you'd like to contribute. It's five dollars a word! Five-fifty for upper case or italics.

EDGAR enters, moping. MAXWELL approaches him.

MAXWELL: Dr Harrington? How good to see you. But you seem troubled. Something on your mind?

EDGAR: No! Well… maybe someone!

MAXWELL: Ah the sweet tortures of love. I'm no stranger myself. (*Beat.*) But it's wonderful to see you here at the Foundation. Why it's almost as if a ghost… Do you know there isn't a day I don't think about your esteemed brother? Such a tragic, tragic loss to genetic science. I was so thrilled to hear that you've been taking up his unfinished experiments.

EDGAR: I'm afraid my research with arachnids is rather amateur. I may look identical to my late brother but alas I've none of his brilliance.

MAXWELL: I'm sure you're being modest.

ESTELLA approaches.

ESTELLA: Edgar! (*Aside.*) What are you doing here! You know you don't have the stomach for this! (*All smiles to MAXWELL.*) Maxwell, of course you know my brother-in-law, Edgar? Well, the twin brother of my *first* husband the late Dr Garston Harrington. Will you excuse us please, Maxwell? Let's meet at the buffet table? I can pick you out something rich, creamy and full-fat whilst we whisper sweet pre-nuptials in each other's ear.

MAXWELL: That sounds enchanting, my dear. (*To EDGAR.*) Good bye, Garston – I'm so sorry, Edgar. (*To ESTELLA.*) The resemblance really is uncanny! (*Exits.*)

EDGAR: It's ready, Estella. I've completed all my tests and the machine works perfectly.

ESTELLA: At last!

EDGAR: We could finish this tonight if only we could find –

ESTELLA: We must look harder!

EDGAR: I've advertised for specimens in *The Clarion*, that may get a result.

ESTELLA: *The Clarion*! We have to keep the press away from this. We've already had a reporter poking his nose in around here.

EDGAR: I saw!

ESTELLA: Don't worry, it's taken care of. Now you find us a spider (*Looking off in MAXWELL's direction.*) whilst your Black Widow goes to work on her next victim. What would fatso say if he knew you were really my husband and it was your idiot twin brother we buried in your place all those years ago?

EDGAR: You make murder sound something to be proud of.

ESTELLA: No, no my darling. What choice did we have? If the authorities had discovered your experiments had gone so very wrong that you nightly mutated into the spider killer, they'd have had to lock you away. How would you have researched reversing the accident then? Faking your death and paying hush money to the victims' relatives gave you the freedom you needed. Who'd ever suspect nice Dr Edgar?

EDGAR: When will this nightmare be over?

ESTELLA: Soon, my love, if your machine is ready.

EDGAR: It is.

ESTELLA: And once we've returned you to normal I shall announce marriage to my late husband's twin brother. Who could quarrel with that?

EDGAR: And your conscience?

ESTELLA: My conscience is clear.

EDGAR: Your heart is flint, Estella. I've changed; I'm not like you anymore. And… I… I… I love someone else. Someone's who's everything you used to be but more. Pure and innocent and generous of heart and –

ESTELLA: Oh Garston, not another one. And have you told this latest bimbo you mutate into a human spider each night at midnight?

EDGAR: I was saving that for our second date.

ESTELLA: Hasn't she noticed yet that anyone upsetting her in front of you ends up as the next spider's victim? Maybe she likes it!

EDGAR: She doesn't think like that. You might enjoy setting my alter ego to slaughter your enemies but she's nothing like you. When did you become so ruthless?

ESTELLA: (*Kissing him.*) You adorable little fool. Wait until we're man and wife again. I'll soon make you forget all your little floozies. Now, time for me to do a little fund raising at that buffet table. I have fatso's new will upstairs and judging by the way he sweats when I'm near, it shouldn't take me long to finish him off.

EDGAR: (*With distaste.*) You're incredible.

ESTELLA: It's all for you my darling. (*She exits to MAXWELL.*)

EDGAR: Leave her! Stop her! Let her kill! (*Calls off.*) Manfred.

MANFRED enters.

EDGAR: Wait until Miss Estella's fully occupied with her latest victim then pay off the young journalist and let him go. We've already too many murders on our conscience. This Foundation used to be a force for good.

MANFRED: Yes, Sir.

EDGAR: And Manfred. Has the new batch of serum arrived to stabilise my condition for a few days?

MANFRED: Not yet, Sir. Perhaps tonight though.

EDGAR: (*Desperate.*) Before midnight? Tell me 'yes', spare me another night as the man-spider freak.

MANFRED: We're doing our best, Sir.

EDGAR: Oh God, another night of horror. More helpless citizens slaughtered by my ghoul-like alter ego.

MANFRED: I'll do all I can to get you the serum before you turn again.

EDGAR: Midnight! I must have it by midnight!

MANFRED: I know, Sir.

EDGAR: Of course you do my friend. But when the Black Widow takes control you're as helpless as every other man on this planet. Call me at my practice if the serum arrives.

MANFRED exits.

In Two Minds

SINCE I BLEW MY TWIN UP AT THE QUARRY
I'VE HEARD HIS VOICE COMPLAINING IN MY HEAD.
EVR'Y TIME I'M PLANNING SOMETHING WICKED
HE MAKES ME GO BE NICE TO FOLK INSTEAD.
YOU'D THINK IT WOULD BE AN ADVANTAGE
TWO VOICES TALKING THINGS THROUGH.
UNFORTUNATELY
THEY NEVER AGREE
ON QUITE WHAT THEY WANT ME TO DO!

BROTHER ONE'S A VICIOUS SADIST
BROTHER'S TWO'S A TEDDY BEAR
I SET OUT TO GO MAKE TROUBLE
AND HE'S YELLIN' 'DON'T YA DARE'.
HALF OF ME'S NICER THEN ICE CREAM
THE OTHER'S A PERMANENT GROUCH
I THINK THEY'RE DELIGHTING
IN CONSTANTLY FIGHTING
OH, WHERE'S THE PSYCHIATRIST'S COUCH!

TWINS, YOU'D THINK, WOULD HAVE A LOT IN COMMON.
WE TWO NEVER DID SEE EYE TO EYE.
HE WOULD STOP TO STOOP AND SNIFF A FLOWER
I WOULD STOP TO CRUSH A BUTTERFLY.
I CHOSE A BRANCH OF GENETICS
THAT, GRANTED, WELL...ISN'T TOO NICE
BUT HE QUITE DESPISED HOW HIS TWIN ANALYSED
TORTURING LAB RATS AND MICE.

He voices both sides of his personality.

NICE: CRUELTY'S UNNECESSARY.
NASTY: DON'T START ON ME WITH THAT CRAP.
NICE: SCIENCE SHOULDN'T MESS WITH NATURE.
NASTY: TAKE A HIKE YOU LIB'RAL SAP.
NICE: I HELPED THE MENTALLY TROUBLED.
NASTY: I BEAMED A SPIDER THROUGH SPACE.

NICE: AND SEE THE RESULT!
NASTY: WELL, THAT WASN'T MY FAULT!
NICE: THERE ARE CORPSES ALL OVER THE PLACE.

AND SO THE VOICES RAGE AD INFINITUM
I'M CRACKING UP, I DON'T KNOW WHERE TO TURN.
NICE: IF ONLY YOU COULD MAKE DELORES LOVE YOU,
SHE COULD BRING THE PEACE FOR WHICH YOU YEARN?
NASTY: ESTELLA'S WORK FUNDS OUR FOUNDATION
AND ALL THE EXPERIMENTS THERE
NICE: ONE OF 'EM MUST GO
NASTY: SO WHICH?
NICE: I DON'T KNOW!
I'M SCHIZO, AND IT'S SO UNFAIR!

EDGAR's consulting room.

(*Calls through a door.*) No more patients tonight, Nurse Emanuel. It's getting late. (*Looks at watch.*) Godammit, it's nearly midnight. You'd better go. Lock the door on the way out, will you?

He closes the door and miserably pours himself a large scotch. The phone rings, making us jump. He answers.

Manfred? The serum's arrived? Oh thank God. (*Looks at watch.*) 11.15. 45 minutes. If I drive like the devil I can be with you before the spider monster takes control of my body. Have it ready. I'm on my way over.

He hangs up. Grabs his coat but is interrupted by the arrival of DELORES. He constantly checks his watch during the following.

EDGAR: (*Panic.*) Delores! How did you get in?

DELORES: Nurse Emanuel thought maybe I could cheer you up.

EDGAR: Well, ordinarily I'd be over the moon but...are you OK? You look kind of upset.

DELORES: Oh don't mind me. Just guy trouble. See, this fellah asked me out on a date tonight and like a dope I said yes, got all dressed up like Joan Crawford in *Dead Men Don't Cry*, butterflies in my stomach you know the kinda thing?

EDGAR: I know the kinda thing.

DELORES: And then, of course, he didn't show up. I felt so lonely, so blue. Where in this rotten city would I ever find a decent man, an honest, honourable man. Someone straightforward and caring with no nasty secrets…and… I thought of you. Your note was so beautiful this afternoon and well… I wondered if you could use some company around the midnight hour. Maybe a cocktail at Zak's.

EDGAR: I… I can't. I can't now. I'm in a real hurry. You wouldn't understand I…

DELORES: (*Bottom lip quivering.*) You're turning me away? You're rejecting me too? I feel like Jan Sterling in *Mystery Street.*

EDGAR: No I… how could I reject you?.. I… it's just, not Zak's, not midnight, you'll have to take a car journey with me. I have to collect something. Something very important. You won't mind that will you? I'm afraid I may have to drive rather fast but… Oh Delores, will you come with me?

DELORES: (*Immediately cheered.*) Sure we can go for a drive. That'd be swell. Maybe you could grab us something to eat on the way.

EDGAR: (*Looking at his watch.*) Let's hope it won't be you.

DELORES: Pardon me?

EDGAR: Nothing, nothing at all. Right. To the car. I'm so sorry you were stood up. Some men have no idea how to treat a lady.

DELORES: The monsters! Thank God you're not a monster, Dr Edgar.

As they leave he looks at his watch.

EDGAR: (To himself.) Oh God!

They leave.

The Black Widow's apartment. JOE is creeping around. JOE looks inside the match box and talks to the spider.

JOE: Hey, you still alive, Harry? Good spider! You hang on in there until we get to the bottom of this. I wish you could see this apartment the Black Widow's got. It's like something out of the *Bride of Frankenstein.* Nothing useful though. In fact I guess I might as well go home and see if Delores is still talking to me. Nothing unusual here at all.

MAXWELl: (*Off.*) Estella!

Uh oh! Someone's coming.

He hides.
MAXWELL enters dressed in a very short baby doll night dress and a baby's bonnet with a dummy in his mouth which he now removes.

MAXWELL: Estella, Naughty Maxwell is ready!

He sings (very Al Jolson).

I Want to be your Baby

I WANT TO BE YOUR BABY, BABY
MAKE ME YOUR BABY TOY.
BABY'S MISBEHAVING MOMMA
OH WHAT A NAUGHTY BOY.

Wind me,
Spank me,
Take me on your knee.
I gotta be your baby, Baby
Feeding time for me.
Rock me in the cradle of your bosom momma
Hold your little baby tight
Or I'll throw my toys 'out 'the perambulator
Ain't going be no settling me when
You wanna get some sleep tonight.
Junior's calling, can you hear me crying
Cause I'm teething and my gums
need something hot to chow
So rock me in the cradle of your bosom momma
Wanna wipe my diaper now?

(*Spoken.*) Estella! Where are you?

I want to be your baby, Baby
Make me your Baby Toy.
Baby's Misbehaving Momma
Oh what a naughty boy.
Wind me,
Spank me,
Take me on your knee.
I gotta be your baby, Baby
Feeding time for me.

Kick line finish.
I gotta be your baby, Baby
Feeding time for me.

Encore (very, very fast)

I want to be your baby, Baby
Make me your Baby Toy.
Baby's Misbehaving Momma
Oh what a naughty boy.
Wind me,
Spank me,

TAKE ME ON YOUR KNEE.
I GOTTA BE YOUR BABY, BABY –

JOE sneezes in his hiding place, interrupting the song.

MAXWELL: Mommy? Baby can hear you.

The fat baby tiptoes over to JOE's hiding place.

Come out! Your honey's ready to suckle!

They freeze.
In the darkness we hear the sound of a car failing to start.
Then of an owl and nightbirds/frogs/crickets suggesting the countryside at night.
DELORES and EDGAR enter in the darkness with torches.
he has a petrol can and is highly agitated.

EDGAR: I can't believe it, of all the time to run out of gas! We're not going to make it, we're not going to make it!

DELORES: Relax, baby! Don't you think it's kinda romantic out here? What a beautiful night with the moon on the tree tops and that creepy old building up on the hill!

EDGAR: The Arachnida Foundation! We're nearly there, we can walk it. OK Move!

DELORES: Honey? Is something wrong? And don't you have some gas in that can?

EDGAR: I thought so but it's chloroform. Delores, we have got to start walking! We have got to get to that building before midnight.

DELORES: Okay sweetie, okay. Keep your hair on, (*Sexually intrigued.*) jeez! You can be quite masterful, can't you? Like Fred MacMurray in *Dance for Daddy*. (*Something catches her attention.*) Oh Dr Edgar look! Did you see the little bunny, I guess they must live all around here, can we just wait and see if there's anymore –

As she babbles on and clearly isn't going to move EDGAR looks down at the petrol can of chloroform he's carrying which has a rag around the handle. She is facing away from him.

Only the other day I was saying to Mr Chandler, a nice writer guy that stays in the hotel, I was telling him, a Film Noir featuring bunny rabbits – *maybe* on a picnic, *maybe* not – is something Hollywood ought to think about. I'm sure it would be very popular. Don't you love the way their little white tails bob up an down when they run and their little twitchy noses –

He pours chloroform on the rag.
She acts out having a bunny nose.

– Sniff, sniff, sniffing! All day long. Say, what's that smell, can you smell anything?

He advances on her from behind with the rag.

It the same weird smell I get just before I have my blackouts. Then I wake up and someone who's been mean to me is dead.

He holds the rag over her face. She collapses in his arms..

EDGAR: And I'll always protect you from the creeps, freaks and psychos of Angel City, my darling. Even if the biggest freak is me. Now I gotta get you some place safe before the spider takes control of my reason and my appetites.

He stumbles off carrying DELORES.

MAXWELL is about to discover JOE behind the curtain.

MAX: Mommy! Baby's coming to find you. Baby wants to play Peek-a-boo!

He pulls the curtain aside to reveal JOE.

JOE: (*Meekly.*) Good evening. I'm guessing you're probably expecting somebody else.

MAXWELL: (*Roars.*) You again! What the hell do you think you're doing here? Estell–

But he starts to have a heart attack.

JOE: Oh my, are you OK? Take it easy there. You're… you need to sit down… I… are you having a heart attack?

By now MAXWELL is lying on the floor and JOE is astride him trying to pound his heart back into life.

How does that mouth to mouth stuff go?

He then attempts mouth to mouth.
ESTELLA enters dressed for MAXWELL's seduction and sees this.

ESTELLA: Get off him! I seduced him first, you money grabbing little… He's mine.

JOE: Miss… Mrs… I'm afraid… I think he's died of a heart attack.

She goes into a extravagant pantomime of grief.

ESTELLA: No! No! No! It can't be true. (*To the heavens.*) Why Lord? Why, did you take him from me so suddenly? We had so little time together!

JOE: It must be upsetting.

ESTELLA: (*Suddenly sharp.*)You bet your ass it's upsetting! He hadn't signed the new will yet. Now every penny'll go to a racoon sanctuary in Vermont. (*She calls off.*) Axel, Manfred. Get rid of this tub of lard.

They enter and take MAXWELL's body out.

Dissolve him in the acid with the remains of last night's Spider Freak victims. (*Beat.*) What on earth am I going to do now? I'm running out of ailing, elderly millionaires.

JOE: That'll make it hard to pay for all that compensation.

JOE and ESTELLA alone.

ESTELLA: Just how much do you know?

JOE: There's still a few pieces missing from the jigsaw. Maybe you can help me figure things out.

ESTELLA: And why should I to do that?

JOE: (*Flourishing the match box.*) 'Cause I brought you a spider.

ESTELLA: Why would I be interested in some old spider?

JOE: Oh but it's not just any old spider. It's hideously mutated.

ESTELLA: Everybody thinks they've an interesting specimen but each one brings more heartbreaking disappointment. So what's the story? Did you break off a couple of the legs on the way over here? You people are pathetic. Is there no depths to which you won't sink for money?

JOE: Well look who's talking, lady?

ESTELLA: I don't have to explain myself to you.

JOE: You do if you want my spider for your research. I'd say it was a pretty unusual specimen. A huge bulbous head, thick hair sprouting all over.

ESTELLA: What! Let me see that?

JOE: I want some answers first.

She pulls a gun.

ESTELLA: I don't think you're in any position to be making demands. Now give me the matchbox. Very carefully.

JOE: You sure are one crazy, mixed up dame.

ESTELLA: Shut up. You don't know anything. How can the world understand the love my husband and I shared before he… The depths to which a love like that can drive you? (*To the match box.*) Is it you my sweet? At last, is it you?

She opens the box and gasps.

Oh my, Oh my. You're finally here. At last you've come home, no more sucking up to fat old perverts. Now we can be together again.

JOE is creeping towards the door. MANFRED appears in the doorway.

MANFRED: Not so fast! (*To ESTELLA.*) Doctor Edgar is coming up the driveway now, Madame. There is someone with him. (*He handcuffs EDGAR to a chair.*)

ESTELLA: I'm not expecting anyone else.

MANFRED: He's carrying a blonde in his arms.

ESTELLA: I've an idea who that little tramp is. Kill her!

MANFRED: Yes, Madame.

ESTELLA: No, no I've got a better idea. We'll have him do it. And I want to watch. You're not to give him that serum you understand.

MANFRED: But how will we control him?

ESTELLA: As he starts to change bring them both up to the tank.

MANFRED: The tank?

ESTELLA: Yes *the* tank. Make sure it's secure.

MANFRED exits.

Soon it will all be over. (*To JOE.*) Well it seems like you'll have the dubious honour of being the last man I have to kill. Tonight is for giants not pygmies.

JOE: Try me. I got a kinda enquiring mind.

ESTELLA: Very well. It seems churlish to deny you a last wish. My husband was engaged in a series of experiments to transport matter through space. Over several years he built this extraordinary machine.

A central panel slides open to reveal a spectacular machine with a very obvious switch/handle with which to activate it.

He would throw this switch and a rock in one tank could be dissolved into miniscule atoms and beamed across the room to reassemble in this tank on the other side.

Another panel slides open to reveal an empty tank. It has a big illuminated arrow inside it pointing to where the machine is designed to beam things.

That alone would have made him a hero of science. But he wanted more, he wanted the immortality of legend. So he tried transporting living creatures. Rats and mice at first, then cats, dogs, monkeys. Sometimes it would work, sometimes the animals would show up hideously deformed, or occasionally not at all and then the next poor creature through would arrive with the previous animal conjoined on to it. It was horrific. But one day my husband knew he'd made the breakthrough he needed.

JOE: And he tried to beam *himself* across the room? To be the first human being to travel through hyperspace. Did it work?

ESTELLA: We thought it had but when the clock struck midnight something terrible happened. My husband began to mutate into a half-man, half-spider freak. The size of a man, the compassionless appetites of a spider. As dawn restored him to normal, he concluded that when he put himself through the process a spider must have been in the launch tank with him. They both came through but with their molecular structures mixed together. Somewhere out there was a spider as mutated as he was.

JOE: Now, thanks to me, you've got that spider back.

ESTELLA: And the machine has been rebuilt so that when my darling and the arachnid go through it again the process will be reversed, each will be restored to normal and I can have my husband with me once more.

MANFRED enters.

MANFRED: Everything is prepared Madame. All that is required is the arachnid.

ESTELLA: Thank you, Manfred. (*She hands him the matchbox.*) To the tank.

MANFRED: The tank. (*He exits.*)

JOE: So there's the messed up spider. Where's your husband? (*He looks at a clock on the fourth wall.*) But I see it's nearly midnight so maybe I should say, 'Where's the Spider Freak'?

ESTELLA: They tell me he's now safely contained in the launch tank with a little snack to keep his strength up. So now we can begin. Behold.

She pulls a lever and a third panel opens revealing a tank on the opposite side of the machine to the tank with the arrow. Underscoring.

Through the glass we see but cannot hear DELORES screaming, banging on the glass and looking terrified over her shoulder.

JOE: But that's not your monster husband, that's my girlfriend! My girl's in there, get her out!

ESTELLA: Impossible I'm afraid. But don't worry she won't be lonely!

Thunder, lightening, dramatic underscoring, the Black Widow crowing with laughter as we see the spider's legs and web begin to entangle DELORES and the horrifying face of the Spider Freak appear behind her.

JOE: No! No! Stop this now!

ESTELLA: And jeopardise everything I've worked for all these years? Never!

A shot rings out. ESTELLA drops to the floor. GRANGER the butler enters with a gun.

GRANGER: Good evening, sir. (*He retrieves the handcuff key from ESTELLA's body and releases JOE.*)

JOE: What the…the servant guy, right? With the compensation.

GRANGER: Mother and I are very fond of Miss Delores, sir. I thought she might need some assistance

JOE: Wow! You're a great shot.

GRANGER: I'm in training, when I left domestic service Hollywood called with a chance to audition for the role of a British secret agent. I can't see such a character catching on though can you, sir?

JOE: I don't see why not.

GRANGER: I don't miss my old profession but I wanted a chance to, just once, look down at a corpse and hear the immortal words –

JOE: The butler did it!

GRANGER: Thank you, sir.

The glass of the launch tank is steaming up obscuring the horror within. Although we can still see movement.

JOE: Now we've got to get Delores out of there.

They throw themselves at the launch tank trying to find a way in.
They don't see ESTELLA crawl over to the control panel, haul herself up and with her last ounce of strength pull the big lever that starts the machine.

Black out.
Fx explosions etc.

Lights up on JOE calmly standing at a lectern.

JOE: Fortunately, ladies and gentlemen, members of the Pulitzer Prize committee, fortunately the ruthless couple had made one more fatal miscalculation. As you read in my prize-winning article, the mutations had become so well established in the bodies of scientist and spider that the machine's attempts to separate them just pulled each of them to pieces, and it was impossible to re-assemble all that molecular scrambled egg into anything. Both died. But I'm happy to say my beautiful Delores emerged unscathed except for a few nasty spider bites in some uncomfortable places, and she and I married a year ago. She sends her sincere thanks to you all for my Pulitzer Prize and indeed the lovely set of steak knives because she's resting up at home. I'm proud to tell you that she's expecting our first child any day now!

Applause.

JOE is handed a note. He holds up his hand to silence the crowd.

Ladies and gentlemen I've just heard I'm the proud father of triplets!

More applause over the blackout.

Lights up on JOE and DELORES (in hospital gown) crossing to a crib.

JOE: Are you sure you should be out of bed honey?

DELORES: Sure, the doctor says I'm fine. It all went so smoothly. Besides I wanted to be here when you saw the kids for the first time. Oh Joe they're adorable.

JOE: I can't wait to see 'em.

DELORES: Oh Jelly Bean, could our lives be any more Shelley Winters in *My Man and I*? You, me the triplets –

JOE: A Pulitzer Prize for journalism.

DELORES: A new set of steak knives.

JOE: So let's meet the gang. Any ideas for names yet?

DELORES: No, I thought I'd wait so we could decide together. Wake up little angels – here's daddy!

Fx. Insect buzzing sound.
Three disgusting human baby sized insect mutants poke their heads over the sides of the cot.

JOE: Aghhhhhhhhhhhhh!

Blackout.

Lights up.

Everybody sings –

B Picture Acting (reprise)

B PICTURE ACTING IS A CRAZY WAY TO EARN.
'WISH WE COULD DO SOMETHING MORE PROFOUND.
THREE WHOLE YEARS AT THE METHOD ACTING STUDIO
JUST TO BE THE BOZOS RKO CAN KICK AROUND.
THOUGHT WE'D SOON PROGRESS BEYOND FILM NOIRS
CAMEOS FOR STUDIOS WITH ONLY TWO-BIT STARS,
BUT THERE'S ALWAYS FEMME FATALES TO FIGHT
IF ONLY LIFE COULD BE THIS FUN
AND JUST AS BLACK AND WHITE.

The End.